Christmas Sermons

Christmas Sermons

Displays of Development in a
Theology of Christian Faith and Life (1790–1833)

Friedrich Schleiermacher

Edited by Terrence N. Tice
Translated by Terrence N. Tice and Edwina G. Lawler

CASCADE *Books* • Eugene, Oregon

CHRISTMAS SERMONS
Displays of Development in a Theology of Christian Faith and Life (1790–1833)

Cascade Books
An Imprint of Wipf and Stock Publishers
199 W. 8th Ave., Suite 3
Eugene, OR 97401

www.wipfandstock.com

PAPERBACK ISBN: 978-1-5326-6739-8
HARDCOVER ISBN: 978-1-5326-6740-4
EBOOK ISBN: 978-1-5326-6741-1

Cataloguing-in-Publication data:

Names: Schleiermacher, Friedrich, 1768–1834, author. | Tice, Terrence N., 1931-, editor and translator. | Edwina G. Lawler, 1943–, translator.

Title: Christmas sermons : displays of development in a theology of Christian faith and life (1790–1833) / Friedrich Schleiermacher ; edited by Terrence N. Tice ; translated by Terrence N. Tice and Edwina G. Lawler.

Description: Eugene, OR: Cascade Books, 2019. | Includes bibliographical references and indexes.

Identifiers: ISBN: 978-1-5326-6739-8 (paperback). | ISBN: 978-1-5326-6740-4 (hardcover). | ISBN: 978-1-5326-6741-1 (ebook).

Subjects: LCSH: Theology. | Sermons, German—Translations into English.

Classification: BV4282 S3513 2019 (print). | BV4282 (epub).

Manufactured in the U.S.A.   AUGUST 30, 2019

Contents

Preface

Dear readers, Christmas sermons are the best place to trace Schleiermacher's focus on Christ's redemption of humankind. This volume features the eleven extant full sermons from Christmas. Each one richly offers views of this great festival, at the same time showing key developments in his theology from beginning to end of his career. Regularly, he addresses the original listeners and readers of these celebratory remarks as "devout friends." The approach is always up front and interpersonal. In effect, they compose continual complements to his fictional, dramatic dialogue, *Christmas Eve Celebration* of 1806 and 1826 (ET, Tice, 2010).

You too are invited to join him in these sermonic dialogues, originally spoken extempore from tiny outlines then revised for readers. Having greatly enjoyed translating Schleiermacher's writings for readers of English over three decades by now, we are seasoned for this task. Born in Saxony, Schleiermacher himself gained preaching skills by translating several volumes of sermons by two noted practitioners of the art in his day: Hugo Blair and Joseph Fawcett. In his day and ours, English has been largely a language of "anglo-saxons." As a major contributor to modern German in his time, Schleiermacher nicely bridged his German language and the language used by Scottish and English speakers then. We are crossing that bridge, in turn, moving from German to current English usage, this time as Protestant and Roman Catholic respectively. We believe that persons of faith from all parts of the one, if still divided, Christian church will find that in many respects Schleiermacher speaks for and to them. Since he intended to reach out to those of other persuasions who were often in his audience of listeners and readers, other current readers might well find something for them in these sermons as well.

If there was ever a single "father of modern theology," as Schleiermacher is widely reputed to be, he would still have to be it in our own day and beyond. This would be true by virtue of his many extraordinary gifts as a preacher, pastor, professor, and public figure whose contributions have been utilized by individuals and groups of many stripes, both religious and otherwise, including so-called postmodernists. Please simply try to think of yourselves as readers wanting to hear more about what Christmas might mean. We aspire to your not being disappointed.

Here are four guides to reading this book: (1) Openly and patiently, let Schleiermacher develop his argument each time. He had about forty-five minutes to finish the task, so that they will all appear to be more like treatises than like the brief colloquial remarks that current churchgoers are accustomed to. (2) Expect different styles and emphases each time, partly because they are based on different New Testament texts and partly because he was at changing parts of one's life cycle when he delivered them and had revised them for a broad readership. He was barely age twenty-two, beginning candidacy for ministry, when the first one came along, and he probably worked at revising it a bit much, even for us. It might help to imagine his loving and expressive face and his age at each point in his life (November 21, 1768—February 14, 1834). (3) Also, let the five Editor's Postscripts offer you successive background information, separately or as you proceed. (4) Take time to "ponder," as the mother Mary did at the time of Jesus' birth; and imagine your taking the role of others related to the traditional scene when Schleiermacher focuses on each one.

Here I am glad also to acknowledge this edition as an instance of a jointly translated works with Edwina Lawler, to which I also take responsibility for adding editorial material. We are both very grateful to Janet Bardwell for her sizable, outstanding and meticulous technical assistance and to staff at Wipf and Stock who contributed to the clarity of expression and the structural appearance of this work, namely: K. C. Hanson, Jeremy Funk, and Heather Carraher.

Abbreviations

ed.	editor, edited by
ET	English Translation
KGA	Schleiermacher, *Kritische Gesamtausgabe*
SW	Schleiermacher, *Sämmtliche Werke*. SW II.2 (1834, 1843)

1

What Interest All the Circumstances of Jesus' Birth Have for Us

Christmas Day
December 25, 1790[1]

But when the fullness of time had come,
God sent his Son, born of a woman, born under the law.
—GALATIANS 4:4 (NRSV)

Prayer

To bring thanks and worship before you, merciful[2] and gracious God, is always our first concern when we gather to draw heavenly wisdom from the source of your revelations and to remember your blessings together.

---

1. This sermon, among three long extant, is in revised form after an early review by Schleiermacher's uncle Samuel Ernst Timotheus Stubenrauch (1738–1807), probably within the 1791–1792 period. It is also from among the few to survive of the many preached during his years as a candidate for ministry (from the summer of 1790 until his ordination on April 6, 1794). He was employed with the very large von Dohna family at Schlobitten in East Prussia, from October 1790, having passed his first theology exam in his native Breslau during the summer of 1790 and having preached his sermon exam on July 15, 1790, at Berlin's Cathedral Church in that city. This Christmas sermon was last revised at Schlobitten during this same period as a candidate. It was first published in SW II.4 (1834, 1844), 34–64, the source used here.

2. In later sermons "mercy" is usually dropped, except in rare instances. For example, it is used with explanation where the biblical text contains it, as in a Christmas sermon from 1824 included here below. See *Christian Faith* (2016), §85.

Especially today, however, nothing must be more pressing for us than this. We would not want to praise you for anything that would somehow enable your goodness to redound to humans in his day. It is the remembrance of the greatest and most priceless gift that you have deigned to give humankind for which we gather here. Praise and thanks to your Son that he became human, that he descended to us, that he did not consider being equal to God thievery; rather, he gave himself up and accepted the form of a servant and became like us in every respect, this in order to bless, or save,[3] us. Praise and thanks to you, O Father, that you have sent your Son to us, him without whom we were lost, and also that you may fulfill the wish of our hearts that this festival too might strengthen us in our faith in Christ, in our love for what is good and in our hope for your further mercy! Amen.

The custom of celebrating a special day of those who are in some way dear to us, my good friends, is established almost everywhere, and this is one of the good and innocent means to secure one more day that is dedicated to true human joy.[4] How joyfully do we not see everything when a family observes a father's or a mother's celebratory day? How, by some mysterious effect of nature, is each mind and heart open to cheerfulness

---

3. In all the translated sermons below, the word that appears here is *selig machen*, meaning "to bless," "to save" (or both)—hence "to bless, or to save." Often elsewhere it is "blessedness" or "salvation" (*Seligkeit*). Here the rudiments of Schleiermacher's theology already show up; in many respects further refinements that remained basic were manifested in signs of his inner faith and of his theologically and scientifically informed worldview before his first pastorate in Berlin (in its General Hospital's parish from September 1796 to 1802). In an increasing development, this worldview continued to gain an organic form, systematic in its details, over the rest of his life. This sermon displays where he always started, theologically speaking, whereas those that follow from 1810 to 1833 were gathering many facets of inner feeling and perception (hence of common understanding), all meant to be shared by himself and the main core of his Church of the Triune God (*Dreifaltigkeitskirche*) and in other churches where he was a guest preacher.

4. This feature too remained in his doctrinal theology and Christmas sermons throughout his life. Naturally, all celebration in the church is intended to foster joy. However, within the church year of his time and place, two periods were especially marked out for this purpose. Christmas and the "season of joy" between Easter and Pentecost were to highlight this theme of joy. One might ask, was this custom the only reason for Schleiermacher? Read on!

and joy far more than otherwise? Each person involved strives to be happy and to make oneself feel happy, and by striving for that state one is already deemed to be happy. One feels oneself to be imbued with love, but one loves far more warmly, far more intimately at such times than usual. Without being conscious of it, the memory of all former enjoyment condenses within one's soul, and in this way we also experience more animatedly and more strongly the love that binds us to this human subject; we have our joy simply in its very existence. For at least just as good a reason, all of Christendom has appointed a day to celebrate the memory of Christ's birth, just as heartfully and just as joyfully as at other birthdays. As Christians we all constitute a large family, and Christ is its head. By means of religion we are united therein, probably not in as merely sensory a manner but in as firm a manner as are members of a family by the bond of blood. A knowledge of truth, a pathway to what is good and to happiness, a faith in God and in eternity—that is what unites us and what we as a community owe to the subject that is Jesus, who is the founder of our supreme happiness.

Our ultimate purpose now is to rejoice in his entrance into the world, but, speaking frankly, on this day we may also ask: Do we feel in proportion just as warmly, precisely what we would feel as children on the birthday of a father or of a mother? I think that only a few among us will be able to say that. When we consider that the one whom we see coming into the world so helplessly and in such an unpleasurable condition is precisely the one with whom diety has united in such a miraculous fashion that in this child God, so very quietly and unnoticed, was bestowing on humankind its sole and greatest benefactor, also that in this nocturnal moment his look of grace, as it were, was smiling anew at the earth, and that in this moment the judgment of mercy was being carried out over the whole world. Yes, when we think of all this, it has to rouse feelings of grateful joy! However, these feelings will ever remain mixed and complex if we are contemplating an event that is as far removed from our capacity as this one is, simply taken as one package. Our feelings would then engage our imaginations more than our hearts, and precisely for that reason our imaginations would be subjected to numerous delusions. This is true especially on this day, when the memory of all the small joys connected with this festival in childhood easily offer a sensory supplement to the heart's feelings.[5]

5. Two major themes are introduced in this paragraph. The first, drawing from one major tradition grounded biblically, is that Jesus came as a servant, living within

Thus, let us use this hour to secure the feelings that we see arising in us today. Let us bring this great event closer to our hearts in that we contemplate all its parts and convince ourselves of the great influence that each of its circumstances also has on us and on our well-being. God, who so gladly supports us when feelings that are so important to us are at issue, will not withhold God's own blessing from us for this effort if we appeal to him for it.

[After rereading the biblical text:] Paul, who in this part of his letter speaks of the history of humankind with a view to religion, very clearly confirms for us what we just spoke of. Since here he is speaking of the great change that Christ's appearance produced within the course that the human spirit had been taking, he is not content to indicate the matter itself thereby. He explicitly calls attention to the fact that all these effects could result only if, in the course of human affairs, all circumstances requisite for them would be managed together precisely at the time of Christ's appearance, and to the fact that he had to be born under certain conditions that relate to the guidance of human beings hitherto and to the later fruits of his sending. Thus, in accordance with the way these words were directed, let us consider *the interest that each circumstance of Jesus' birth must have for us* and then also remain *with the feelings and sentiments[6] that are engendered within us by these reflections.*

---

a lower-class family. It is rare, however, to find interest in this low status expressed in so many details as are emphasized here. The second theme derives both from inward-tending factors present in his Herrnhuter Brethren, Pietist background and, in revised form, from his own investigations into psychological factors within human beings, especially in religious life but streaming out to other inner- and outer-directed functions of the self. In the second aspect, emphasis on "heart" (vs. intellect or understanding) betokens an early effort to move toward a clear focus on inner faith, to be distinguished from any directly belief-grounded faith (the same word, *Glaube*, having to be used for each form). We will see further ways to explain the internal-to-external and communal functioning of inner faith in subsequent Christmas sermons, notably when the term "feeling" is used. See Tice, *Schleiermacher* (2018).

6. "Sentiments" would seem to refer chiefly or solely to the sensory domain, which would speak of and somewhat qualify the feelings (*Gefühle*) that are the focus of this sermon by the young genius. By this time he had begun to form a psychology that would distinguish several levels of mental functioning—here at least involving sensoriness and some sense perception vs. a higher level of feeling and perceptual functioning—thus inner faith versus domains of cognition and of knowing and believing. "Disposition" (*Gesinnung*) is an alternate shade of the meaning covered by "sentiment." It is usually the meaning chosen in this edition of sermons.

I

Each person is destined to contribute something in one's life to fulfillment of God's designs, and within each one lie the seeds for everything that any given person will be for the world, in the position wherein one is placed into the world at the point of one's first step, in the land that educates one, in the time in which one's existence falls, and in the conditions that surround one. Not one of these circumstances is fully present in the case of Christ, but they were all necessary if the purpose of his sending was to be fulfilled completely and in such a way that we would also participate in it. We see Jesus being born among a people whom we can perhaps never really and fully love as such, whose heart is impenitent, whose character is perverted, a people always ruled by vulgar passions of every sort, people for whom to imagine Christ's spirit and Christ's nature would be embedded in the grossest contradiction. He had to have suffering to live among human beings who unceasingly rejected him from childhood on, and who, already in his first days, began to persecute him. God had given this people God's promises, but these had come to be subordinated to superordinate designs. It was the people of the Lord, yes, but all peoples were equal in the Lord's eyes, and only his wisdom[7] could determine where Christ was to live. However, this people of Israel were, first of all, the only people from whom it was deemed possible to have an influence on all of humankind. Even if religion was perverted and misunderstood among them, it had a proper foundation nonetheless. Therein, religion was important to each person. Therein, it was possible to instruct many and to win over many for a better truth. Only among this people could Christ

---

7. Here Christ's wisdom seems to be the primary category, whereas in *Christian Faith*, (2016), §§164–69 (1830–1831) it is secondary to love among God's most clearly evident attributes. This can be explained in that Schleiermacher is relying chiefly on Christ's teaching to manifest Christ's redeeming character, whereas, at least by the period when he was forming his dogmatics lectures, we see affirmations of Christ's own love showing up as the primary element of his communion, or community, with God and with persons and congregations composed of persons bearing inner faith in their loving relations to him. This period had begun by the time Schleiermacher had taken a post as preacher and teacher in Prussia's University of Halle in 1804. It culminated in developments of his theological work at the University of Berlin from 1809 (before its official founding in 1810) to the publication of a first edition of his doctrinal (versus ethical) aspect of his two-volume doctrinal dogmatics in 1820–1821. This was followed by his greatly revised, second edition in 1830–1831. Nonetheless, this sermon already carries more characteristic marks of post-Enlightenment thought, despite this lingering mark of a typically Enlightenment focus on wisdom.

be the popular teacher whom we have come to love, the teacher who gathers human beings around himself in large crowds, proceeds based on the truth that they all have in common with him, and in this way continues to lead them on its path. Among this people his teaching could take root and be maintained. Among all other known peoples religion almost amounted to a collection of mere superstitions, and it was at least separated everywhere from the heart and ordinary life for human beings. In such a condition it would have been impossible to remove all inertness and all firmly rooted errors for religion to thrive over one lifetime and to enter into such eccentric human souls with pure truth. Given that condition, the teaching of Jesus—just as the lesser wisdom of so many lights of antiquity did—would have died along with a small circle of better friends, and nothing of it would have remained to us.

However, one also sees in the example of the first Christians into what kind of trouble those who had accepted the teaching of Jesus would have come if later on they would have received knowledge of God's older revelations. Were they to reject the one for the sake of the other or unite the two with each other? Here freedom, there slavery; here gentle wisdom, there hard if majestic strictness; here love that draws us to itself, there fear, also fright that knows how to bend a person under its yoke so easily. What a difficult choice this would have been for a person filled with doubt, for one who would always fear that one might take the pathway to what is good too easily and would thus prefer wanting to believe and to do everything so as not to miss anything! However, Christ, born in Judea, left us with no doubt as to what option we must take: He showed us what we have to think of this older religion: He taught us to distinguish laws regarding the human soul from the particular reign of an uncultured, imprudent people. According to our text, this is what Paul says in his words to the Galatians, who were not completely in agreement among themselves concerning this contrast. Therefore, Christ had *to be born under the law* that he might save those who were under the curse of the law that they might receive adoption. We would always have wavered in our knowledge, and our faith would have been divided between two distinct revelations of God. In order to calm us concerning that duality and to make us wise, in order to cancel this conflict that arises from knowledge of two revelations, our blessing or, salvation, had to come from among the people of Israel. Only in this way could we survey all paths taken by the Lord in a series, in an unbroken connectedness.

Yet, this people also had their better times, times of peace when observance of the law became a source of happiness and of satisfaction in view of that happiness, times of greatness when under persecution, they knew how to die with courageous enthusiasm for the law. Yet, neither of the two options was attaining the upper hand by the birth of Christ. Reserved to him who loved his brothers and sisters so deeply, who simply wished to see them good and happy, was heading only to feeling their perdition and seeing before his very eyes their own imminent ruin. *It was not granted to him to be witness to their happiness and to their virtue.* From the first moment of his life onward, he had to sacrifice even this wish to the certain success of the teaching that he was to proclaim. Only in these last years of his nation was the time of his appearance fulfilled. Would he have found belief in Israel if he would have demonstrated the incompleteness of the Mosaic law at a time when the people were thereby peaceful and happy, or would such listeners have properly understood the faults of this law at a time when giving up one's life for this law would have been the greatest of honors? The first Christians, who were from the tribe of Israel, were still adhering even then to the ancestral law, and if they were to deserve their name justifiably, even the last hope in themselves for an exclusive advantage of their nation would have had to disappear. They had to see their own state ruined, their social bonds dissolved, and their sanctuary irretrievably destroyed. Likewise, Christianity, to the most essential advantages of which belonged being a universal religion for all human beings and being known for that, could not be restricted for long within the narrow circle of this small group of people. Moreover, it also could not be thoroughly founded earlier than shortly before dispersion of that nation itself, at a time when it was already forced by all the circumstances it was facing, to end the separation that had existed hitherto from all other human beings. Thus, Christ had to appear *only under this people, only at this time* if he wanted fully to attain his goal.[8]

---

8. What we might have seen just now as a dire interpretation of Israel's religious situation when Christ appeared (also as an unnecessary one), Schleiermacher did not emphasize in later years—surely not after the early years of the nineteenth century, when he wrote a friend that he intended to know Paul as well as he knew Plato. Here, however, following Paul's contrasts, Schleiermacher articulates and argues for a view of Old Testament religion that could be termed hypocritical. Nevertheless, Schleiermacher never used Old Testament texts for sermons except for public, civic occasions, and he constantly held that adherents of this religion would have to go through a process of conversion or transformation just as so-called heathen (Gentiles) also would, including as well as other purported monotheists. See *Christian Faith* (2016), §§11–14

Yet, in what kind of a situation do we see Christ make his entrance into the world! The magnificent tribe of David, from which he had descended, had sunk to the deepest, most unknown obscurity, and Jesus was born and reared in a condition that probably left only a few members of his people below his social status. His first moment was a picture of his future life. He was born without wealth, without property, without a homeland, and he also lived in this way. Not the slightest trace of external nobility distinguished him. No prospect of comfort and prosperity sweetened his first days. Nevertheless, my friends, even this was necessary for the benefit of all those who were to gain faith in his name. Above all, Christ could not and did not want to have an influence on the rich and the distinguished of the earth, because they would be incapable of following him. Hence, he did not become a rich and prominent man. Rather, he thanked God that for the present he might reveal his wisdom to people of lesser estates. He wanted to make an impression on the hearts of a larger number of people. For that reason, he had to deign to become like them, for every day we do indeed see that people can feel neither confidence nor love toward those who have all too many external advantages over them. They bear only envy, admiration, or indifference toward those who are specially advantaged. Moreover, what excuses does a person not find in one's heart if, in the case of one's enjoying external happiness and lack of trouble, that person, for whom virtue itself might seem to be less difficult, might give others rules for achieving virtue. Ah, only a few would have had faith if Christ had occupied some grand spot in the world! For that reason, he preferred to be poor, humble, and suffering from the first moment of his life. He wanted to be tempted by all human misery, so that he could show us all the more perfectly and convincingly how one can overcome all temptation through vigilance and prayer.

Let us add one more reflection. If Christ had to be a real human being in order to redeem us, then we too have *to imagine his soul to be just like ours*, also subject to cultivation of and orientation to education and to all the circumstances that can otherwise have an influence on one's soul. Thus, under any other people, at any other time, under all other conditions, Christ would not have been the one who he is, nor *could he indeed be any greater or kinder* than we see him to be. Nowhere could the outstanding aptitudes of his spirit, which was to climb the highest steps to such perfection only by means of adherence and love to divinity

---

and §108. He preached only two other sermons on this text, on December 26 in 1795 and 1802, none later.

and its commands, be formed better and more splendidly than among a people who, despite their perversion, had indeed directed all established customs to creating for religion entrance into a young heart and for making its motivational grounds more powerful than anything else. This was occurring at a time when the contrast between law and the conduct of those who accepted the contrast itself had eventually to reveal to its hasty judgment all deficiencies and errors with which humanity lay afflicted, and also had to draw the contrast ever more firmly toward true and simple wisdom and knowledge. Finally, Christ was born and reared in a situation wherein thousands of wondrous circumstances had strained the heart of a tender and pious mother, so that she could direct all her attention to the delicate plant entrusted to her, where no storms from outside would disturb his younger self. Rather, peaceful, quiet, and domestic solitude would leave time for his soul to develop and to ripen toward the great destiny that his soul was to fulfill.

II

So, what follows from all these considerations for us? Simply this, my friends, that each circumstance that relates to the birth of Jesus is extremely important for us, that these considerations were all necessary for accomplishing his destiny. Further, how much must this reflection increase our participation in everything that coincides with the subject of our festival today! Everything, even the least thing, ceases to be a matter of indifference for us. The land, which was actually dedicated to the bliss of a pious peace, wherein from childhood on he could see and know all the places where God had evidenced God's miracles to the people of Israel, where from childhood on he could wander among the quiet abodes of pious fathers whose corrupt descendants he, in turn, wanted to return to the path of simple wisdom, the native town of his great ancestor David, which was also his native town then. The time in which he could open his eyes for the first time, a time of error, of general deterioration and horrible vices, in the sacrifice of which he himself would almost have become like an innocent child, a time when defiance and weakness of a divided people would predict imminent misfortune and would serve to encourage the young soul to hasten and to effect what is good before further darkness would come. All particularities of his own situation (this nightly stillness, this restless predicament of a mother who was traveling, away from home), which details had to make so much of an impression on her heart and had to increase her love and attentiveness so much! She had seen the deference of the wise men; the admiration of the shepherds, who worshiped him without knowing him; the persecution of the evil prince; and the ecstasy of the old Simeon! Everything that Mary preserved within her true heart becomes important for us, because, directly or indirectly, it has an influence on Jesus and on his character, because it all had to come together in order to make him into that which he was supposed to become!

In my soul, my friends, a great augmentation of my love for Jesus arises therefrom, and I believe that this will be the case with all of us, for it seems to be so very natural. We always love a matter that is quite important for us all the more, the more we feel how easily we could have missed it, and this is precisely the case with Jesus. The more important he is for us, the more easily some circumstance that would have afforded him a completely different course could prove otherwise, so then the more extraordinary guidance of providence would be necessary, from his first moment on; so too all the dearer he would become for us, and all the more would our love and our affection for him begin to mount. All the more would we be participating even in the first part of his life, all the more fully and fervently would we be rejoicing *that he is and that he is there precisely as he is!* We would feel the needs that we and the entirety of humankind have had and have been inflecting afterward, so that we rejoice twofold *to see all our wishes so richly satisfied in him*! And, what sort of wishes! A fallen human being would also have lost *the measure of strengths* that one would no longer be using. Then one would no longer know what one was to do; in fact one would no longer feel what one could do. At that point, one would not long for someone from among one's own kind in whom one could become distinctly aware of how far a human being could move along the path to perfection with God's help! In all these situations, Christ was born for us, Christ who as a human being also possesses the perfection that is ordained for us! In that role, he is placed as proof of how completely like us he is: He has flesh and blood as do we, he is weak and helpless and powerless, he runs along the same path trod by every human being in his development and growth of strengths, and he presents to us his special example, viewed as the highest triumph of human nature!

The unhappy person would also have lost *one's relationship with God*; God's love and grace would have disappeared for each such person, and each one would need a new and splendrous proof of that love and grace in order to awaken from one's deadly dream. At that point, God sends us Christ, who restores for us everything that we have lost, who permits us to gain strengthening insight into God's own character, and, as a sign that we can trust Christ, that God is with him, and in that his discourses bear truth, actually the most excellent proofs of divine cooperation[9] accompanying his entire life from the first creation of that life!

So, how should we not rejoice in him who restores the glory of God, brings heavenly peace to humanity, and spreads a gentle pleasure over the entire earth!

Yet, let us not breathe out in vain even this beautiful feeling of joy, which joy is the distinguishing character of this festival. When we become aware of something good that lies within us and for us, that is, when we are rejoicing, then we are always most inclined to contribute something to making this goodness even more our own and to use it. Christ is present, and we rejoice in that, but let us also take care that he is present as much as may be possible for us.[10]

Editor's Postscript

This sermon shows much of what Schleiermacher had arrived at during his residence at Schlobitten (1790–1794) and during the final two years of candidacy for ministry (aged twenty-two to twenty-four) and a pastoral charge in Landsberg an der Warthe until September, 1796 (ages twenty-six to twenty-seven).

What should be added here lies in parallel to his attempt to offer "considerations," or pieces of an account, regarding Christ's own background and his mature movement into ministry here. It also presupposes Schleiermacher's own distinctive journey heretofore. For one who has investigated this second story, which is ordinarily constructed from fragments, I would point out that resources are available for the work of a serious biography of Schleiermacher's own younger years. Earlier writers have suggested this—chiefly Wilhelm Dilthey (1870); various collectors

---

9. See *Christian Faith* (2016), "divine cooperation" in the Analytical Index.

10. Here the original text contains this note: "Conclusion is lacking." See *Christian Faith* (2016), §12.

of his immense correspondence, especially Kurt Nowak's thoroughly re-searched study (2001); and briefer swats at details throughout the Schlei-ermacher literature since his lifetime. At this juncture, I simply attach the following features to this first Christmas sermon, focusing on *Elisabeth Maria Katharina*, born Steubenrauch (1736–1783).

(1) Schleiermacher's Mother

What Jesus might have achieved with his mother we've heard about here. About all we generally hear of Schleiermacher's mother is that she was devout, bore three children and died (at forty-seven), but more is to be said. Here's a start. He was essentially in her care over fourteen years after his own birth in Breslau, on November 21, 1768 in Silesia, in East Prussia. He was a second child by three years after Charlotte (Lotte), who their mother often put in charge of him; and it is fairly well known that when Schleyermacher (how the family name was then spelled) was seven years old, Lotte had smallpox (which left her face and body very scarred). It is also known that these two siblings constantly remained closely in touch with their mother throughout their young lives, until she died in 1783, at the age of forty-seven. They remained very close with each other in adult-hood, until Lotte died, unmarried, in 1831. Their younger brother Carl (born in 1772) is still outside his elder brother's story, though after a trip over mountains to see Carl Schleiermacher reports a rather constrained life by this *Apotheker*, but a "lovely, happy [marital] household." Another account tells of a large gathering of relatives and friends in 1813; so far I do not know how long Carl lived, but there can be no doubt that they were all dearly loved by their mother, whose husband had to leave all household affairs to her but "instructed" the children on rare, brief stays at home. The special gifts of her elder son had to have been discovered very early. Since her own birth family had been in highly placed, well connected, Reformed-preacher-households, in touch with each other over several generations back, they would have pitched in with resources geared to his gifts, and she was sharp in her own right to arrange for this. Otherwise her talented son would have been left free curiously to wander and find, to wonder and absorb, during his first five years. The public school available at age five was adjudged to be so inadequately run and so narrowly focused after brief attendance as to lead him to be negative toward such schooling phenomena as he had experienced them with an active mind of his own in subsequent years, and to regard other resources in households and elsewhere in society to be promising prospects for teaching and learning. This interest, shown through his writings and his example, placed him among Germany's most cited progressive educational theorists well into the twentieth century. This reputation was due to his mother most of all, in my estimation. This particular son tried valiantly to gain approval from his largely obdurate, demanding father Gottlieb (1727–1794) right up to the father's death at age sixty-seven. However, Gottlieb lived too much "away," as it were, to have much influence on the directions the son was to take in his life. By his first university years, his mother's preacher-professor brother, Samuel Ernst Timotheus Stubenrauch (1738–1807), took Schleiermacher into his home and stuck by him until this uncle's death at sixty-nine in 1807. No doubt Schleiermacher's mother also had a momentous influence on his widely touted friendly character: He was respectful of all, with an open-hearted and open-minded manner of working things out with people holding diverse opinions. By the time Schleiermacher had reached around ten years of age, his mother and her own birth family of Steubenrauch, not so much his mostly absent father, would have assisted his efforts to form his own values over an extraordinarily wide spectrum. Both of them would have supported his forming a set of special needs and interests necessary for moves toward his forming his own "distinctive identity" (his concept). In sum, much more is yet to be told about his family situation and environs well into his teens. However, the main thing to be said of his upbringing until age fourteen and a half is that his mother lovingly attended to the large range of this unusually gifted child's growing needs and interests for the entire period, up to his entering puberty, including to Schleiermacher's strongly egalitarian and protofeminist tendencies. His half sister Nanny, was the eldest of three daughters brought into his father's second marriage in 1785. During some of Friedrich's bachelor years at Berlin, then at Halle, she had headed his household. She later assisted in child-rearing within Friedrich's household from 1809 to 1817, the first half of his marriage. Once Nanny married in 1817, with her he entered into the von Arndt, von Brentano and von Arnim circle in western Germany. The Steubenrauch family included notable Reformed clergy. For several generations back, its high reputation afforded it social standing such that few besides well-placed pastors and aristocrats could form sizable libraries, thus, these relatives were able to assist the young Schleiermacher's early education. When he attended the University of Halle as a lad, he is known to have taken great pleasure from living in his uncle's study, which was stocked with books, some no doubt already familiar. His sister, who is known to have helped with the two younger boys and in the household generally, shared some of her brother's interests.

(2) Books and Libraries

His mother and her distinguished family had the wherewithal to look after his arising need for proper books. Similar to a practice arising in the fifteenth century, Guttenberg's Germany had been providing collections of printed matter mostly lodged in family libraries of well-off citizens. In this case, Uncle Steubenrauch would likely have been Schleiermacher's main source even for children's literature, though he later reports a temperamental "skepticism" toward the fabled accounts of "flora and fauna" that was typical of such literature when he was still a small child.

(3) Enlightenment and Pietism

This sermon's *knowledge-related language* shows some lingering influence from the then still current German Enlightenment, though his emphasis on one's heart and inner faith also displays influences from other thinkers of that eighteenth-century period, strengthened by five teenage years of experience in pietistic Herrnhuter Brethren schools. During and before Schleiermacher's lifetime, dozens of distinct pietistic movements were to be found among the German territories. Periodic literature has continued to focus on their history since Martin Prozesky's monumental 460-page dissertation on the subject at the University of Rhodesia, "A Critical Examination of the Pietistic Element in the Religious Philosophy of Friedrich Schleiermacher" (1976). This study deserves to be fully updated, for it points to a variegated, powerful movement coterminous with the Enlightenment within European and American environments to a movement that is markedly present throughout Schleiermacher's continuing influential work, not only in his theology, but in his considerable philosophical work as well.

(4) Conflict and War versus Communal Living

As a career military servant of the Prussian king, Schleiermacher's father, Gottlieb (1717–1794), brought into the family a profound consciousness of ravages wrought by belligerent social conflict and war. The son, Friedrich, was to serve the king and people during periods of war and French occupation in Prussia (1807–1813), as a booster (one offering encouragement and solace), and also as a political reformer and a cofounder of new educational institutions, also finally as one critical of political encroachments into church matters. When invading armies threatened at the gates of Berlin, he even marched in the streets alongside defending soldiers, this without carrying a gun.

2

On Participation of a Good Person
in the True Well-Being of Humankind

Christmas Day
December 25, 1791[1]

Now there was a man in Jerusalem whose name was Simeon; this man was righteous and devout, looking forward to the consolation of Israel, and the Holy Spirit rested on him. It had been revealed to him by the Holy Spirit that he would not see death before he had seen the Lord's Messiah. Guided by the Spirit, Simeon came into the temple; and when the parents brought in the child Jesus, to do for him what was customary under the law, Simeon took him in his arms and praised God, saying.

"Master, now you are dismissing your servant in peace, according to your word; for my eyes have seen your [blessedness or] salvation, which you have prepared in the presence of all peoples, a light for revelation to the Gentiles and for glory to your people Israel."

—LUKE 2:25–32 (NRSV)

---

1. This sermon first appeared in his first collection of sermons (1801), a major early work to be ranked among a succession comprising *On Religion* (1799), *Soliloquies* (1800) and these *Sermons from 1789–1794* (1801). All these sermons were written out after delivery at the country estate of the von Dohna family (named Schlobitten) and sent to Schleiermacher's maternal uncle Samuel Ernst Timotheus Stubenrauch (1738–1807), a preacher and onetime Halle professor, for comment, then further revised. This one is closely related to a New Year's sermon of 1792, in ET, ed. Lawler, *Fifteen Sermons* (2003). It later appeared in SW II.7 (1836), 117–34, the source used here.

16

When Jesus' apostles wanted to give the Christians, who were directly en-trusted to their instruction, a quite strong impression of their Redeemer's good actions, they said to them: No one has greater love than this, that one would lay down one's life for one's friends.[2] In contrast, he died for us when we were still enemies,[3] when our souls were still wholly removed from the dispositions in which he has preceded us. Moreover, my dear friends, he suffered for us, when we did not exist at all. However, we need not stop with his suffering. His entire life was a life for others. This is so, for, far removed from attending to his own happiness, the entire course of his life aimed only at disseminating among humankind the divine truth, which was entrusted to him from heaven. Yet, he never did have the joy of seeing the success of his efforts among good folk, in that he was misun-derstood and misjudged, almost universally so. Moreover, a good growth of the seed that he had sown was to be expected no sooner than at a time when he was no longer alive and among people who were never actually present to him and about whom he knew nothing save that they would be human beings as he was. Thus, what would have been capable of induc-ing him to constant perseverance, given such a life, if he had not been inspired to have an elevated feeling of warmest, most widespread love of humanity, of the most extensive benevolence[4] directed toward all those who would share a human nature in common? Viewed as his inheritance, this exalted feeling rested on his first disciples, who traveled to far distant nations without being in any closer relationship with their own people, that fearing their ignorance and their aversion, simply for the purpose of proclaiming to humankind the truths that Christ taught and the com-mandments that he proffered. Moreover, he also recommended to us this very same feeling with the words that we should love one another as he has loved us.[5]

So it is, with us, for whom this commandment and these examples are sacred. There can be no question of whether this exalted feeling, love,

2. John 15:13. Schleiermacher paraphrases, alludes to, or exposits biblical material in his sermons, and the translators and editor have honored this. On a few occasions the NRSV is directly quoted, as indicated.

3. Rom 5:8, 10.

4. To the end, the basic characteristic of love Schleiermacher always emphasized was that of willing and extending what is good, benevolence with regard to human beings. For him, the resultant state of being is not always or necessarily happiness (well-being). See notes 6, 7, and 11 below.

5. John 13:34.

might simply consist in our having had available to us only those who did not really know what it is to have a human life, thus whether this feeling might be merely an exaggerated tension of the soul, wherein it can be sustained only for brief instants at most. Yet, alongside this reflection one wish that we do feel is that there might be many occasions for us to retain and to animate this disposition, in view of the fact that within the circle of ordinary life this disposition finds little encouragement. This wish arises, for life's various relations do indeed serve to bring people closer to each other by dint of mutual needs, so as to foster many connections of friendship, of goodwill, and of mutual interest. Thereby, we also find ourselves being moved to nurture the social inclinations of the human heart. However, the more closely we associate in these ways with a larger or a smaller number of people like ourselves, all the stranger do certain others come to be for us. At the same time, all the less would we then retain feeling for those other people with whom we bear no particular relation. Accordingly, by means of good and noble feelings that we surely do have for those other people, feelings that we should have toward all people gets lost, namely of the most general, most unlimited benevolence toward humankind.

Yet, how would we not want to strive to unite the various groups of acquaintances with each other? How dear would not love of humanity come to be for us if we should reflect further on its nature and its value? Moreover, what could enjoin us to engage in this additional reflection, or what could bring us to be more skilled at it than this very day! Everything extraordinary and of a more widespread nature, which, in turn, leads us toward elevating ourselves above what connects us simply to our particular relations, also leads us to some greater conviction. Indeed, where is something more extraordinary and more nearly universal than the good deeds that were poured out over humankind by the mission of Jesus? Thus, we will certainly turn the festival of Jesus' birth to good account in its hours of worship if we rouse ourselves to the disposition that constantly ruled within him, and by which he came to be everything for us.

Suppose that we imagine what motives stirred the pious old man Simeon to such outpourings of joy and to such an exceptional emotion of his heart when he was holding the young Savior of the world in his arms. We would then easily see that these moods cannot have been due to his own need. During the period of Israel's old covenant with God, he was one of the few wise men who stood out within their own era. He was a wise man who was truly devout and pious, despite errors that had captivated the people of Israel. He was a wise man who could grasp something of the knowledge that Christ was destined to spread more widely among humankind, and he was one who would have been comforted by it. That he held this child in his arms could help him but little, for, alas, he would surely feel that his own advanced age would rob him of any hope of being Jesus' friend in Jesus' own adult lifetime as a teacher. It would rob him of hearing gladsome instruction and sayings from his lips. However, in everything Simeon says, he aims at blessings that all of humanity would enjoy through Christ. His joy lies in his viewing the one who was to bring all these teachings and blessings about, so that when he should depart from the earth he could look at his coinhabitants with the most joyous of hopes. Accordingly, we are speaking of a good person's interest in the true well-being of humankind, and here we see, first, in what this disposition of love would consist; and, second, what it would assume that would exist within the soul; and, third, what sort of good it would bring forth within the soul.

I

Now, supposing that we do look into the question as to the nature of this general benevolence,[6] we must first notice that we often ascribe to it much that actually proceeds from completely different sources. Not every good rendering of service that we exhibit to someone with whom we are not in any close relation is to be derived from this disposition. We generally

---

6. This entire sermon offers an initial analysis of love, defined as essentially a will, or desire, for what is good directed toward another person or all persons (including oneself) or to God and thus also experienced as from God. This definition and its corresponding disposition or orientation of self is a permanent, brilliantly shining jewel in Schleiermacher's treasury of ideas, both psychologically and theologically speaking. Because he has already identified his relationships such as friendship, in which benevolent love can occupy oneself, readers are free to consider whether the analysis points to a special kind of love or to a basic condition of all loves, and of every kind. If it were to be the latter, then the term would represent a pro-attitude, perhaps an opening of self to its personal objects, or subjects, as it develops and moves toward or gains perfection, as it reaches consummation, or in some fashion represents most precious values (goods) in life. For an earlier contribution toward the present analysis of love among his works, once the 1792–1793 essay, wrought during his pastorate at Landsburg an der Warthe, *On What Gives Value to Life* (1995); and his other long-unpublished early philosophical essays related to fundamental features of human life (most notably freedom, development, and "the highest good"; also on happiness and well-being). See also "love" in *Christian Faith* (2016), Analytical Index.

give in to either a feeling directed toward doing something good, a feeling that arises in and presents itself to us, or to a benevolent disposition that we find within ourselves. Often we also simply want to avoid the displeasure that the sight of certain pains or lacks of pleasure gives us. No moreso do certain other feelings belong to this group, even if they are spread over a great number of human beings. Thus, often blameless and good feeling does indeed include a partiality that most people have for the country where they were born and raised; for the people among whom they live, and in whose protection they enjoy each amenity of their situation. Irrespective of closer social connections, others, in turn, also have special wishes and remarkable enthusiasm for those who are similar to themselves by virtue of their knowing certain religious truths, or by virtue of their being attached to the same opinions. This too is natural, and even if it does immediately give way to many abuses, in itself it is not to be summarily dismissed, nonetheless.

However, in general terms neither kind of disposition belongs in any way to our universal benevolence toward humankind, for these feelings relate to a number of persons whom we otherwise consider to be better and more fortunate already. Furthermore, if we are always striving to provide even more advantages for them over others, then the latter condition might indeed naturally come to be ever more strange to us, and their partaking of our benevolence might also diminish. In contrast, true love of humanity is always full of the wish that those of our brothers and sisters who still remain behind with respect to enjoying many aspects of well-being that might be possible for them become more nearly perfect and both have and give joy. These elements of their spirit's rise toward perfection that might be brought closer to them as much as possible and such that in this way our joyful participation in their lives might also be increased. If Simeon had thanked God only for the elevation of his people, his feeling would still have been noble, but in no way would it have been a model of this disposition. To the contrary, he actually expresses, sooner and more strongly, his joy over the light to arise for and among the Gentiles, who were, to be sure, still more unfortunate and needy than what stirred his joy over the glory of the Israelite people.

To this is added that love of fatherland or of persons holding faith in common. Moreover, such feelings always have a considerable role to play in our own well-being, for the splendor of the people to which we belong, and the reputation and fame of those who are of one mind with ourselves does reflect on us to a certain extent. It does directly increase our comfort, satisfy our self-love, and flatter our sense of pride. That universal benevolence, however, is a feeling of a sort that in no way depends on satisfaction of any inclinations we may have, or of on any advancement of our own happiness. Rather, it is a feeling that fills the heart with the unselfish but nonetheless lively and almost uninterrupted wish that everything called human, everything that shares in our nature, might increasingly approach its destiny. Thus, it was this feeling that grounded Simeon's thoughts when he was looking at the world around him. This feeling contains the point of view to which he was referring all events and all actions of human beings—that the reign of passions and of harmful errors among various peoples might decrease, that what is good might get to be easier and more customary for them, and that a knowledge of sublime truths that refer to religion and to virtue[7] might come to be more widely disseminated among them.

Moreover, in this very respect, how close to this man's heart do his brothers and sisters not lie? He need not even move out of himself to become aware of dispositions that arise in one's love of humanity. Should one of the beautiful feelings, or even a fruitful consideration of cold reason, have strengthened him in an otherwise difficult, good act and have helped him accomplish it happily, oh how warmly would he then wish to be able to share this aid with all those who dwell in the same situation

---

7. Arguably, the primary focus in Schleiermacher's writings on ethics over several decades (quite separably philosophical or theological, as to their respective grounding) lay chiefly in virtue, not in duty or in identification of ideal ends. As this critical realist would claim, the third, ideal-oriented category erroneously presupposes having exactly in mind what an actual end would amount to, this before the actual full development toward the ultimate general destiny or, specifically, the reign of God toward which humankind may be tending and may eventually reach in full. Thus, in both domains he does have a teleological ethics in this case one tending toward an eventually experienceable state (*Telos*). "Virtue" denotes especially, almost literally, via inner "strength," thus force (*Kraft*) expressed in action (*Handlung*). In theology this approach to ethical issues, given the circumstances and points of development in his era, is done in a carefully juxtaposed division of his Christian, church-oriented dogmatics into doctrinal and ethical theory. Both are directed especially to practices of leaders in churches, practices especially taken up in the details of "practical theology." Alternatively, they would also be taken up in what his philosophical account would term his "worldview" (*Weltanschauung*) and its general consequences in practice. I would term his overall worldview as one that is, in large part, theologically determined, for he does not leave out concerns that would belong to what he called "the true church," a prophesied entity toward which all religions appear to be tending. He never systematically delineated his general worldview, instead focusing much of his research that would be regarded as pertinent to that take to developments in theology itself.

where he lives! Suppose that at this point he had succeeded, by some pious or good change in his thoughts, in resisting a temptation to which he would often have been subjected, avoiding an otherwise customary mistake by any awakening of some force within his soul! How his humanitarian heart would have immediately asked for the same heavenly blessing for all similarly afflicted individuals! Suppose too, at a time when a previously unseen connection would have made a truth clear to him, or would have exposed an error concerning which doubt and lack of surety would have distressed him until that point, and would have brought many a dreary hour into his soul, many a wrong action into his life— then how gladly would he have been a voice for calling attention to these things among all whom he could reach, as well and for shedding a ray of light on a previously dark corner of their souls! Then what joy would each such report not have given him even if it were only from a some good and noble devout person who had not been known to him before! Even without enjoying this other herald's friendship, even lacking any hope of fully knowing the baby that he was holding, Simeon was sincerely rejoicing then and there, because he was considering this other herald (as would any other individual might also present) to be a treasure of humanity, one who would also be active in doing his part for the baby's improvement! How would he not be rejoicing in each and every humanitarian action now presenting itself to him! His good heart would always be showing him all the baby's fine results, widely scattered if only in presentiment! How every spark of light and truth that he imagines shooting off in some direction or other would be captivating him, for, already in advance, he would always be imagining the bright shine that would eventually spread in sparks around itself some day! How exultant he would be whenever love and enthusiasm for what is good were to exist among some society of human beings that had previously been controlled by other desires! How jubilant would he be over each association of good persons for the advancement of what is good!

Suppose, further, that he should become aware in viewing how widely spreading motives would still stand wholly in the way of love's expansion, and in many circumstances suppose that he should become aware of both how the false glimmer of earthly goods and the all-too-great value generally accorded them would cause human beings to fail to appreciate their true well-being and thereby to give honor even to the most petty passions. Or suppose that he should become aware of how a fantasy that is not kept in check by understanding so frequently might well lead one from the simple truths of religion to the dreams of fanaticism, of how base selfishness, on the one hand, and culpable turpitude, on the other, would still contain the darkness of superstition. Oh, how he might long then for strong aids commensurate with the depth and range of such general evil! How might his spirit take some pains, only to find some possible change during a course of caution, whereby the aids could be engaged; how might he wish to see the day when such a star of blessedness or salvation would rise, and what kind of ecstasy might he feel when he—even at the edge of the grave—might catch sight of its first rays.[8]

This was the nature of Simeon's existence. Thus, in accordance with what we know of him, we must conclude that he was also like this on other occasions. If he was so happy with his way of thinking and with his honest practice of virtue, oh how often might he have wished then for the capacity to spread this disposition among all humankind! If he had overcome one weakness after another over his many years, how often might he then have prayed that even those whom he saw spinning around themselves in more than one weakness might soon be made receptive to this great help in confronting states of human misery, receptive to the support that comes from a pure and true religion! How Simeon might well have rejoiced if here and there—but of course this could happen to him only rarely—he should meet a like-minded person, inspired by the same principles of virtue and piety! How happily he might have imagined the descendants who would be brought up by his agency to the same way of thinking! What sort of feeling might it have been for him when he heard, as it were, from one of the pilgrims who came from distant lands to celebrate the high feasts of the people in Jerusalem, that even among the Gentiles, whose misfortune would have seemed so saddening to him, there were persons who at least followed their better natural feeling and

8. Using mostly the metaphor of darkness vs. light suggested in the biblical text, this part of the sermon has clearly presaged the distinction between sin and grace, which was to organize both editions of Schleiermacher's *Christian Faith*. It is also evident, moreover, that already here for a gospel-oriented Christian person, one who is joining in a collective consciousness of sin would depend on one's having joined in a collective consciousness of grace. See *Christian Faith* (2016), §64 and §§90–92. That work invites one to consider doctrines presenting divine grace, together with sin, itself valued by virtue of divine grace, as alone genuinely Christian doctrines. In contrast, the introduction offers a general framework within which genuine Christian doctrine is to be found. Part I presents familiar but incomplete doctrines regarded as at best preliminary to those contained in Part II and in the Trinitarian Conclusion. Simeon thus represents both a first respondent to Christ among wise and loving Jews and a prolepsis of what can come of living the life of a Christian.

who loved what is good to the extent that they actually knew it! This person, who with such fervor now thanked the Lord for Christ's appearance, how often might he well have been in the same temple to implore and to call down upon humankind all the great blessings that he believed to be possible only by the Lord of all! Even in that brief moment when he was holding the Christ child in his arms, how distant would the fulfillment of these hopes have seemed to be, but how close would it be to such a person of faith and how ardently would it have affected his heart, full of love for humanity!

All other good that such a humanitarian could carry in one's heart for human beings would refer only to this longing for their true spiritual improvement. It is indeed true that one cannot form such definite wishes for the happiness of humankind as a whole as one can for the well-being of the few whose entire situation one knows more exactly, especially any such impossible wish as that all of humanity could arise within us without suffering and misfortune. Besides, mere earthly happiness also cannot be the highest, unconditional wish even of a truly good human being, either for oneself or for others. Yet, when one nonetheless experiences for oneself what a satisfying sense of peace one's soul could enjoy in attaining a certain degree of some relative well-being, and what fine fruits this peace could also bear toward its true happiness, how one's peaceable soul could actively maintain the beautiful feelings of effectual thanks to God, how such a soul could bring one's heart to the point of exhilaration and fill it with gladsome courage, how that soul could enable one's heart to be open to and eager for everything good—oh, in this way, it would indeed come to be natural to wish that this satisfying peace should be spread among all humankind!

When we ourselves feel or see in others what sad consequences certain kinds of oppressive suffering tend to have, how they do depress the soul, surrender it to a dull despondency and dull all its strengths— oh, how would one then wish that the greater part of this suffering that human beings heap upon themselves or upon one another might be diminished! We would then surely welcome each and every discovery of the human spirit that brings forth new sources of well-being! Blessed is anyone who succeeds in finding new ways for human beings to draw more means from their very existence as well as more fruits from their due diligence, so as to restrain oppressive neediness! Also, blessed is anyone who succeeds in finding new healing powers of nature to free oneself from hitherto overpowering evils! Blessed is anyone who does as much as possible in one's social circle to spread further̖ beings in every way! Moreover, when one sees the sad, widespread sources of earthly indisposition a... how at one point they hinder themselves regarding prong piness by their thoughtless ignorance, how at another po... for happiness is taken from them by unjustified suppressio... should one not long that evils so unworthy of humankind m... appear well nigh banished within the reign of God!

II

So, my dear listeners, this fine disposition of universal love for all humanity is shown in every possible way. One might think, however, that much that cannot belong to each individual human being does belong to particular expressions of humanity.[9] One might bear, for example, a certain particular indifference to being able to be concerned so exactly about what is beyond us and our very closest relations, a certain comfortable standpoint from which one could simply overlook a portion of the world's events and a standpoint that is indeed peculiar only to certain classes. One might bear a certain cultivation of the soul by receiving information for the purpose of judging the well-being versus evil of human beings, this in accordance with certain principles that we might entertain. To do this, however, would produce a mere semblance of reality. Suppose that Jesus' disciples had been free of their own concerns simply for themselves; would they then not still be so often lacking as what was

9. This section too draws from a both general and special theologian's expertise (information and skills) that Schleiermacher had obtained from his psychological and ethical inquiries over the decade 1791–1801 while this sermon was being revised. Both his sermons from this period and his succession of philosophical essays from this same period bear evidence of key advances in his theological outlook, from the ecclesial side and from the scientific side. These advances are chiefly methodological and definitional aspects comprising what he later discussed in the Introduction to *Christian Faith*. These resources for understanding early developments in his theology have not yet been thoroughly deployed in the literature. Their imprint, however, has frequently been retained in the 1801 published version of this sermon—actually too often for every instance to be noted here. Similar characteristics can be detected and sorted out in the first and early revised editions of *On Religion* (1799, 1806) and *Soliloquies* (1800, 1810). Not all traces have disappeared in subsequent revisions of these two companion works in 1821 and in 1822 and 1829, respectively. The first collection of sermons in which this one appears was never further revised but was simply supplemented by later collections, all quite popular.

...ieir work, and would they not also still experience ...ive in danger of losing their lives? After all, are they not ...the most numerous and most unheralded class of people, ...it information did they have beyond that which both natural ...erstanding and the experience of ordinary life affords every human ...eing? In like manner, the old man Simeon, about whom our text speaks, was also distinguished simply by the attributes of his soul. In regard also to his interest in the well-being of humankind, this interest depends not on anything that affects it so far as we know, but such an interest depends for us simply on the nature of our disposition when we participate in what we can experience, and the interest also depends on how what we observe from our standpoint actually moves us. Thus, each and every individual can participate in this love of humanity only if what grounds this way of thinking is found in any individual's soul—where alone it can be found. What, then, is this grounding?

First, it is above all a generally benevolent heart, a soul that is capable of the feeling that is so especially inherent in a good person, namely, the feeling of being pleased with what is good beyond oneself and of promoting it gladly. So, should anyone ever be so burdened with worries, and should there be such adverse relations in one's life, that this unselfish feeling could be totally stifled? I think that we can scarcely imagine a situation like that. Rather, each situation would involve being adroit at supporting this very feeling, because in its own way each situation does bind us to humanity in various ways. No, benevolence itself supplies the very grounding of the human soul, and nothing can overthrow it unless we would have destroyed it ourselves. Moreover, in one who is benevolent there also lies the capacity to be raised up when one is supporting this exquisite feeling and lets it grow to the point of universal benevolence, this by an expansion of what one might already have a glimpse of. Yet, to be sure, for the individual whom nothing external attracts but what already exists within oneself, for the individual who has come to such a lackluster degree of callousness as to find enjoyment only in one's own pleasure—this one finds something to complain about only in one's own pain and is indifferent with regard to everything else. For this individual, even the word *humankind* would describe nothing. This individual would love only one's small ego and would be even less capable of feeling anything regarding the weal or woe of the whole species that is not directly seen, in that this individual would not have any concern even for one's neighbor.

Second, a proper judgment regarding what is universally good for human beings also belongs to this overall benevolent concern. No one who lacks this capability can attain to true love of humanity, not even given the most seemingly benevolent heart. Suppose that a given individual should seek the well-being of human beings defined only in terms of external advantages and earthly joys. Then, this individual would necessarily have to wish ill for many others, in that this individual would wish good things for a few individuals, and thus this individual's feeling could never extend anywhere close to what is universal. Suppose that someone were to seek the well-being of all human beings in an observance of restricted, one-sided, false principles and rules of life. Not only would this individual often contradict oneself in one's wishes for the well-being of all, but this individual would also necessarily consider the greatest number of human beings to be incapable of such happiness. Even without this negative outcome, however, this individual's love of humanity would soon get cold from lack of nourishment. This would be so, for in that this individual's calculations regarding the well-being of humankind would be completely different from the designs and ways of a Supreme Being, only very infrequently and by chance would anything of what this individual would consider to be necessary actually occur, and a feeling of this kind would soon have to be suppressed if it were not supported by fortunate success and by the joys that such success would afford. Yet, should it indeed be impossible for anyone to attain to this knowledge though it were deemed to be so necessary for a love of humanity? Should a Christian be at least able to complain about its being difficult to attain, a Christian for whom what is necessary for a human being is so clearly indicated?

Even so, the presence of this knowledge is, to be sure, not yet sufficient. In everyday experience we would so often have seen that someone's will inclines to something totally different from what one has recognized to be good. In such cases, the best rules might well be contracted for one's understanding, and yet one's heart would be struggling against them in a vacillating fashion. For this reason, we must set down a third requirement, namely, in order to attain to this disposition of love for all humanity, a knowledge of what affects the essential and true well-being of human beings must not exist only in one's head; it must have passed into one's heart as well, and it must have worked hard within one's heart and must have carried a certain tranquility into one's heart. What can happen is that even given the most correct knowledge of that in which the true good of the human soul consists, one's heart would nonetheless be full of earthly wishes that occupy first place within it. In such a case, one's heart could be too greatly occupied within its own social circle to be able to place itself so far outside itself as to include all of humankind. At this point, too many other human beings would be stretched so far away from this circle, that one's heart could scarcely so generally love all of them too for their own sakes. This can happen if one's heart is distracted by all sorts of passion, so that it is caught up in a movement that is too unsteady and too uneasy for such a peaceful disposition to occur within it. Suppose, however, that this same knowledge—this same interest in virtue and religion—were simply that to which everything in one's heart related; then this knowledge would have come to be as alive in one's heart as it had been clear in one's understanding. Then, also the universal wishes for others that would have arisen therefrom would go beyond the paltry wishes of earthly enjoyment in and of itself. Moreover, even if those wishes were to concern the dearest thing that we know in earthly life, they would always leave enough inner peace in one's soul to grasp with one's most active interest the very best of humankind, which would, in turn, refer to religion and to virtue.

The devout old man Simeon who was mentioned in our text was like this.[10] Far removed from being indifferent toward everything around him and referring everything only to himself and far removed from feeling and wishing only for himself, he rather had a certain indifference toward himself and toward what could still be in store for him. His heart burned only for others, and benevolence filled his entire soul. Far removed from seeking in earthly things what was best in those he loved, like many of his time he did not wait for a messiah who would raise the earthly fortune of his people and would place them among the leading nations of the earth. Rather, he waited for the actual Messiah, who would light up all the world, by whom the thoughts of many would come to be known and purified. Far from still being a game of intense wishes and passions, Simeon's waiting brought precisely this happiness of which he spoke—one composed

10. For Schleiermacher, Zechariah, this father of Jesus' cousin John the Baptist, though not to the extent of the wise, old Simeon, might also seem to be somewhat of a precursor and to carry presentiments of subsequent Christians. In particular, Simeon surely was so for Schleiermacher. Simeon spoke in the temple at Jesus' naming, while holding the baby Jesus in his arms—spoke of what he was to bring in his adult years. It would appear that Simeon also bespoke Schleiermacher's own Christian experience and rather divergent experiences of others' living within the scope of the church's inner and outer circles. See *Christian Faith* (2016), Analytical Index.

of an understanding that properly judged the most significant of subjects, a heart joyful to behold. Through this Messiah, moreover, God would instead have spread an enviable peace over his soul. No desire was disturbing his heart. One wish alone was still inspiring him now, the granting of which he was now enjoying, and which lay simply in the most beautiful outburst of his own love of humanity strengthened by the steadfastness and peace of his own heart.

So, in this way we see that each and every Christian is capable of this disposition, commended to us by Christ. We also see that it presupposes no certain external condition but indeed a universal and firm tendency of a heart directed to what is good. Just so, the degree that we find this love of humanity within us, we avoid the separate need of a measure for some uttermost, essential attributes of a Christian mind and heart. That is to say, the more often and the more warmly you feel yourselves moved by such a separate measure, the more insight into what is good is already present in your understanding; and the more benevolence in general moves you, the more love and eagerness for what is good is already present in your hearts. In contrast, the more coldly and indifferently you think of the state of human beings in general, the more surely you are still lacking in one of these three items.

III

Moreover, a benevolent disposition that already requires so much good also cannot possibly be unfruitful. It must also necessarily bring forth many sorts of good in the heart of anyone who gives way to this benevolent disposition, and this is how it is also present.

First, that disposition certainly has the beneficent influence on us that accompanies every feeling that raises us up to something beyond our close relations. It gives the soul a strengthening tension by which it gradually becomes incapable of any anxious concern and of any worry as well as of any jubilant and exaggerated joy over things earthly, things by which it receives a certain composure regarding all occurrences. If one bears such a great object of participation, one that so often and so strongly engages one's soul, then one can then endure more easily the fact that the smaller, less significant objects are rather remote from us or have undergone a change from everything that is earthly. Simeon was like this. One sees this characteristic in the peace with which he was awaiting death, in how calmly he also knew how to bear life with all its changes.[11]

However, far from this disposition, and given life's making the responsibilities of life less important, it rather gives us new incentives to fulfill even the smallest responsibilities if they were to be undertaken with marked diligence. If many who truly want what is good are nonetheless so lazy and nonchalant toward others in practice, this is because they do not recognize everything that is in this respect good and dutiful to be both good and dutiful. Suppose that they are in a situation of being able to render a service to someone with whom they have no relation or whose relation with them does not require precisely these features, and if they are in a situation of exercising a duty of love toward this other individual, perhaps a duty that tends to evoke a mere minimum of thanks. Then, the thought that it is not their concern to attend so exactly to this other individual might well restrain them. On the other hand, one whose heart is filled with love of humanity would also feel a constant striving truly to do as much as is possible for any and all human beings. This individual would imprint this same stamp on all actions. For example, this individual would always seek to perform actions by which something for others who live within one's social circle could be done. It is not necessary

11. This three-part disposition now takes up the final part of a repeated, trifold investigation of God, self, and world in each major set of doctrines in *Christian Faith*. Each of these sets of the three features is both complementary to the other two and organically juxtaposed with them. Correspondingly, in this sermon the main linking conception is that of love's willing what is good, viewed as originally willed and thus automatically enacted by God specifically in and through Christ. In turn, within *Christian Faith* this conception has taken on triune form, examined in the conclusion of that work at its apex on a flowing line of capstones. The imagined history of the wise old man Simeon elevated, at least strongly inspired, to a redemptive experience of communion with God while he was in the temple holding the baby Jesus in his arms. So too is the consummation of the divine Spirit's history with humankind in self and world presaged here. Thus, in effect, the third section of this sermon offers a prototype of God's activity as divine Spirit maybe deemed to be Supreme Being in the Christian church. In *Christian Faith* doctrines of the Holy Spirit make up by far the largest portion of that work; renditions of *Christian Ethics* are focused entirely on actions in and through the Christian church, viewed as a community of faith founded and sustained by Christ, given his intimate relationship as Son of God the Father Almighty. A great many sermons suggest psychologically informed accounts of Christian ethics at the level of more individual functioning as well—something left for others to apply to an as yet nascent discipline of Christian ethics. See *Brief Outline* (2011) §§223–31.

that someone be directly connected with the doer for all duties to be fulfilled by a given individual or by a Christian. The doer would hasten to
be of service, simply because the other individual is a human being, and
on each occasion each of these individuals might well think: How good
it would be for humankind if I always, if everyone always, acted like this.

The noble disposition that we have been considering, moreover,
increases our gratitude and submission to God,[12] and it gives us countless
opportunities to praise and glorify God. Why does it seem to many as if
good human beings were so scarce? Why do they find good actions so infrequently? The reason is that they so seldom attend to or search for such
things; also that being attracted to other things, they pass by good human
beings and good actions more indifferently, and then, when something
reminds them to analyze the state of the world in this respect, they do
not recollect having seen anything of the kind. On the other hand, the
individual whose heart is imbued by love of humanity bears nothing
more urgent than to inquire about whatever good is present in the world.
Throughout this inquiry process this is the first object of one's inquiry.
Such an individual knows that nothing could actually seek to make a big
stir, but one realizes instead that often a good action is to remain concealed. This sort of individual pursues what is good all the more eagerly,
and one also realizes that in a great many good human beings one does
not discover seeds of virtue and piety or rays of truth. This sort of individual always finds the state of the world to be better than others do, and
so one both praises and gives thanks where others only let complaints be
heard. Why are human beings always full of bad judgments about their
brothers and sisters? Why does so much of what they do that is truly
good turn out to be misjudged and considered to be bad? The reason is
that they, not being sufficiently attentive, establish their judgment after
how things appear initially and, based on an inclination to assume what
is bad to be true, are satisfied with this initial appearance. This is the case
especially when that initial appearance shows them something disadvantageous. In this fashion, precisely this lack in attentiveness misleads them
even in their judgments about God's ways, which to them often seem to
be disadvantageous for human beings because they themselves do not
also absorb these ways in their own completely interconnected nature.

12. From at least here on, Schleiermacher consistently held thanksgiving to
lie at the very essence of Christian prayer. The only strict complement to gratitude
that Schleiermacher ever sets forth thereafter is what he calls "calm acceptance." See
"prayer" in *Christian Faith* (2016), Analytical Index.

A true humanitarian, on the other hand, might seem to take for granted much too much in all of this activity, whereas one might well be satisfied with a comparatively cursory glance, and so the humanitarian might often find to be good and useful what others have considered to be bad and imperfect.

Based on this comparison, a peculiar equilibrium then also arises between such cases when divine wisdom truly is concealed from human eyes and when we cannot become aware of the good that divine wisdom intends therewith.[13] When others stop at an individual's undeniable imperfection, there a humanitarian would take comfort from a surely present, even if unnoticed, advantageous reference to the whole. In this fashion Simeon, without being disturbed in his peaceful state, prophesied to Mary that Christ would also be a downfall and an offense for many who dwell in Israel.

These are the fine fruits that we have to expect and await if we tend to and nourish the delicate seed of human kindness in our hearts, and on this festive day we have the finest encouragement toward attaining all of that. When we will have finished investigations into our own hearts, when, with good intention and thankful praise, we will have concluded our inquiry into what, of all the goods that are present in us, we owe to Christ's appearance and into what our very souls would have come to be without Christ, then let us also direct our glance further to what the whole of humanity will have gained by this appearance. "Honor to God in the highest, peace on earth among human beings of goodwill."[14] We will then grasp how true knowledge of Supreme Being has thereby already spread among a great portion of humanity, to what extent the disposition of love has thereby come to be firmly planted amongst them, to what degree humans have come to be happier and more fully satisfied!

This is the festival that concerns a love that is extended to all humanity. It is this event that most signally calls us to that love and elevates us by it. How should we still be afraid in any earthly manner? The God who

---

13. To an informed, keen observer, by this point in Schleiermacher's formation of a systematic theology an account of divine wisdom is almost bound to follow an account of divine love, as in the case in *Christian Faith* two and three decades later, and with the same recognition that comparatively many signs of wisdom are likely to remain concealed; whereas, in terms offered by Schleiermacher, signs of love tend to be more immediately registered via human relationships.

14. Luke 2:14 (NRSV).

gave Christ to us will also give us all things in and through him.[15] How should we still be in doubt concerning God's wisdom if, on occasion, Jesus' teachings seem to be misunderstood? Rather, we would always call out: At what depths God's wisdom and God's love do dwell! The one who brought about this arrangement will also bring forth as many blessings as possible through it! How should we still be indolent in facing what is good? Our very soul would rise to follow in the footsteps of him who loved human beings so very highly as he did! On the day of his birth, let us vow always to act with this worthy disposition at the very least within our own circle! Let us fulfill with joy his dearest commandment, that we should love one another just as he will have loved us! Amen.

15. Rom 8:32.

3

Concerning the Union of What Is Human and What Is Divine in the Redeemer, How His First Arrival on Earth Brings It to Our Clearest Perception

Christmas Day
December 25, 1810[1]

> Who, though he was in the form of God,
> > did not regard equality with God
> > as something to be exploited,
> but emptied himself,
> > taking the form of a slave [servant],
> > being born in the human likeness.

—PHILIPPIANS 2:6–7 (NRSV)

1. This is among twenty-one sermons from 1810 that a certain Professor Matthisson wrote down, edited by Adolph von Sydow. It initially appeared in SW II.7 (1836), 566–74; and in ET: De Vries, *Servants of the Word* (1987), 36–42. The apostle Paul had introduced this apparently earlier hymn with lines in verse 5: "Let the same mind be in you that was in Christ Jesus," followed by a long hymn that was put into verse form in the NRSV. This is apparently the first Christmas sermon Schleiermacher preached after taking up his post with the Reformed congregation at Dreifaltigkeitskirche in Berlin in 1808, and in that year he began lecturing in theology even before the university's official founding in 1810. Since the text of the sermon is unusually short, it was likely recorded more as a précis than word for word. It bears the marks of authenticity, nevertheless.

As varied as the relationships and references of our festivals to Christ are, my friends, each one is nonetheless centered in Christ. This is so, for the one aspect opens heaven, the other aspect illuminates the earth; the one aspect represents the intimate bond that is to unite all persons in forming one community, whereas the other aspect refers to what is individual in a human life, to the need of each person's heart. However, the Redeemer is always the actual subject of our festive feelings, and this is also how the meaning of the festival that we observe in these days appears.

When the great event is narrated to us, namely saying that a heavenly light was radiating from the divine child, who was born in the night, each person finds oneself in a frame of mind and heart that is difficult to describe and difficult to understand. This is so, for it is not only the future blessing, or salvation, that we catch sight of in the child; it is not only the one who would later stand before us so that was perfectly manifested in him, whose features we spy out in the child. Rather, in a special devotion distinctive to each and all, we also feel drawn to the child himself, and we are aware that no external account would satisfy the devotion told of, so that we always find in our hearts something deeper that we would like to express, such that something not comprehended and incomprehensible lies in this scene, in which all our thoughts come together. This happens, in that, as I assume this state is comprised of our shared communal feeling, I want to direct our reflection to the reason for this special feeling of piety and devotion. By this feeling we find ourselves to be affected in our face-to-face experience with the child Jesus.

Precisely that to which the apostle calls our attention in these words, when in Jesus Christ the form of God and the likeness of humans are united in a special, higher manner, precisely that occurrence also contains the reason for the particular pious, or religious, feeling that fills us in these days. At whatever other time of year and in whatever other form we might like to observe the Redeemer—whether in the course of his mission on earth or in the very moment of his final consummation—nowhere do we see what is purely human and what is purely divine so simply accommodated to each other, and we never see so clearly each of these two characteristics, in and of itself, so clearly, than precisely when we are gaining a notion of him at his arrival on earth.

It is this subject with which we want to be engaged in devotion today.

I

Where do we find what is purely human? We find it in Jesus Christ, who though he was in the form of God, did not count equality with God a thing to be grasped but took the form of a servant and was born in the likeness of human beings. Moreover, we are conscious of this, my friends, for how else could we understand the blessing, or salvation, accomplished by Christ? There is indeed something divine in humanity itself, but what is the earthly destiny in accordance with which this divine element was making its appearance? What is the human character for the sake of which the Redeemer divested himself of glory in the way he did? First, its content lies in that the human aspect, irrespective of anything divine within it, nowhere satisfies itself, and in that it appears to be needy when viewed from all sides; and, second, in that what is divine within it, also being under the law of time, develops only gradually and in distinct degrees. Moreover, we become aware precisely of this earthly destiny he bore, which destiny he does have in common with us, in such a very clear way when we move toward him, the newborn child.

Only very little of the earlier period that belongs to the full story of his life has been retained for us, only a few features of his childhood, and then complete silence follows until he appears as an accomplished divine teacher. No matter where we find him engaged in this mission, there, comparatively we would never be able to get a sense of his earthly and human lot, or destiny, so clearly. That is to say, this person, who proclaims divine teachings, who makes the blind see and the deaf hear, who cures the sick and awakens the dead, how could anyone see this person going about in an externally lower form? Even if he would not actually disdain having a social life among only a few other persons, and even if he would let himself be served by them, to the degree that he would also offer help, he himself seems to be in need of none. This person, who founded a new order of things, by whose behaviors and effects the old would have passed away so that a new heaven and a new earth may emerge, who at the same time bears within himself the picture of a new world and form of human existence, who seems not to have received that earlier assistance by which we might progress in what is good, and from which we might derive what good we do have. Yes, a radiance of divine holiness does rest even around those who are similar to the Redeemer, albeit more in the intention underlying their effects than of their disposition, people who appear to be great benefactors of humankind only in certain matters, who by their doings and effects do, to be sure, also contribute to a new divine order but who are guided less by some higher cultured picture of things than by their being maintained and carried by divine intention and necessity only as servants and instruments of divine providence.[2] They might even carry a slight aura of divine holiness about them. In contrast, how much more does divine holiness flow around the Redeemer himself! Moreover, in him the divine and human aspects intermix to such an extent that we are hardly able to separate them. However, let us step back to the first hours of his appearance. Then we see him being like other human beings, having flesh and blood exactly as other children do and, in precisely the needy form, especially in need of earthly love and care! There we feel that he truly has become our brother, that he has become a human being.

Likewise, from the moment our Redeemer appears as such, when he takes upon himself the office of teacher,[3] when he pronounces the great message that the reign of God is to come, when through a few zealous human beings he founds a more intimate union for establishment of this reign, from this moment on he appears to be one perfect human being. We are not in a position to perceive an increase in his knowledge; it is always the same image that hovers before his soul, and when he does not reveal it in crystal clear words, he indicates that he is withholding something because they could not yet bear to hear it. In him divine wisdom and divine understanding are just as perfected as are divine mercy and love. Now, let us also step back to his first lodging, let us view his earthly birth. Suppose that we want to know what to make of him, and suppose that we do not want to view his existence as an empty appearance. Then, we must admit and feel that he developed just as gradually as we do, that the eye of the spirit opened only gradually for him, and that gradually he attained to consciousness of divine powers that were effective in him, just as we too must do. For this reason, we rejoice that he was born a human being, and in such a distinctive way. For this reason, we feel his likeness with us as a truth, as an authentication that he has become our brother, a human being like us, born with the same nature and under the same circumstances.

---

2. In 1810 Schleiermacher seemed to be willing to use this historically vexed concept, at least viewed as a familiar one for use in sermons.

3. This theme of the two aspects or characteristics of one personal nature in Christ is also featured in his 1821 Christmas sermon, through differently analyzed.

II

However, second, let us also strive to perceive in the picture of his child-hood what is distinctively divine that dwells within him in the fullness of its purity. When we then ask ourselves what is the distinctively divine characteristic by which he always distinguishes himself from us, we cannot seek it in what we might view as a guarantee for us as well, namely, that we would be of divine descent. Rather, on the contrary, we must ask: What are the nondivine characteristics that cling to us all and from which we can never completely extricate ourselves?

First, it lies in the fact that in our neediness, in the necessity for the guidance and love of others for us, the possibility arises that what others must do for us could also happen based on wrong motives and in a corrupted sensibility and that, already in this way, a mixture of the higher spiritual motive with sensory and selfish motives[4] would take place such that this mixture is not compatible with a purely divine mode of existence. If in the time of early childhood and from then on through the entire period of impressionable life when sensoriness tends to predominate over what is spiritual, when in this period human beings are affected based on personal, vain, and selfish motives when something external is formed and planted within oneself, this external source already sows itself into one's soul, a source viewed as the seed of earthly components, a seed that will not, in turn, refrain from shooting up and from bearing fruits of corruption.

Further, it is also the case that in our gradual development of the powers lying within us we actually never do keep the right measure or the right pace. Instead, most of our progress in what is good or evil arises by our fluctuating between the one side and the other and in such a way that, at the same time, sensoriness always predominates. Hence, it is unavoidable that, at the same time, what is evil also develops along with what is good, and formation occurs both of reason and of sensoriness. Conflict between the two factors then arises from which we can never completely find the end of it.

4. The contrast laid out here and the terms used to express it had been advanced in Schleiermacher's discourses since the early 1790s. They point to an extended process of intensive psychological inquiry that was probably nascent in early childhood but that delved into new sources and conversations and produced fresh meanings and associations from his middle teens onward. The entire account regarding this contrast, developing interest has yet to be given, though in various publications I have contributed anticipations of one.

Finally, it is that very sensoriness—if by its preponderance it ever presents even the notion of divine force—brings forth particular actions in which we miss the imprint of the divine image. Indeed, sensoriness engenders a habituation to endorse only actions in which features of the divine image are defaced. To be sure, it is also the case that to a certain extent what is divine itself has a part in this corruption, in that not only do sensoriness and reason hostilely struggle against each other, but also thoughts accuse each other among themselves. It is also true that the seed of ruin falls into a human being's very understanding, that one comes to be a victim to that deceitful art of imagining justice to be injustice and vice versa, and even to the art of falsifying justice under the form of reflection and discretion.

All of these habits and behaviors, my friends, comprise the ungodly nature from which no one is completely free. However, it is precisely in contrast to this ungodliness that we find the Redeemer to be free and pure throughout his being and his life. Because of this difference from us, moreover, to us he appears to be incapable of this ruin not only in the days when he had reached consummation, or perfection, but already from the very beginning of his existence.

If we imagine the Redeemer under the care and concern of his own people, can we envisage that an ungodly love was watching over him, that something impure and pernicious was lodged in his mother's love? Viewed in a brighter light, does she not appear to us to be a splendidly pure soul and removed from all vanity, observed as she fully gives herself up to being the handmaiden of the Lord? Then he would have been initiated into life under sacred presentiments and prophesies by divine messengers who, in turn, would have had to inspire minds and hearts with pure devotion and with pious, or religious, expectations. In this manner, he was appearing to his own people from the very beginning on as the anointed one, as the divine servant and ambassador of the Lord God, and it would have been only such a devout love, a love directed at what is of higher estate, that would have brought him up.

Suppose that we then imagine the Redeemer just as we previously thought of him in his purely human relations, likewise gradually coming to be aware of his powers. Then, would anyone be able to believe that he would ever abandon living by the proper measure, that the original relation in the inner ground of human personal existence, a relation between light and divine peace within us humans (on the one hand) and sensory force (on the other hand) would ever be beclouded within him for an instant, that anything simply worldly would ever be placed ahead of the spiritual and heavenly aspects of his life? In his very first appearance on earth he would be seen to be the complete human being in all its purity, nothing of foreign corruption adhering to him, nothing pernicious being implanted within him, and in this way he would appear to us as the heavenly child, as the holy youth, as the completely divine mature man, one always to be viewed as the Son in relation to the Father. Moreover, where do we see this divine purity of human nature more definitively and more satisfactorily than precisely in that what was divine in him was pure and constantly maintained itself, in that within him the human heart was innocent and was never defiant or despondent, so that within him a struggle between reason and sensoriness would never occur, no contest among or between his thoughts. Moreover, this impossibility of what is higher within him being displaced would be precisely why no description and no presentation of his characteristics would satisfy us. We would find that something is missing in it, that he possesses a radiance, a purity—something standing for the perfection of the image by which we have been created would still be lacking in us, and we would carry all this only in our feelings.[5]

Well, my friends, since the Redeemer became such a human being, to the point of having humbly descended into the community of everything human in the highest sense and thereby also maintaining purely that which is divine, nonetheless, so let each of us be disposed just as Jesus Christ too was disposed. May taking in his humbled status become our elevation, his sacrifice our blessing, or salvation. Let us satisfy ourselves

5. In no way can this sermon be interpreted as in support of a long-lasting traditional interpretation of the "two-natures" doctrine of Christ, that is, as if they were both of coequal status, totally human and totally divine. In fact, Schleiermacher combines several mutually consistent affirmations here: (1) God is present and active in the truly human Redeemer's being and life, inside and outward tending. (2) The Redeemer's relation to God is not that of being another and equal Godhead in himself. Rather, what is divine about Christ's earthly existence from being a baby onward lies in the purity (sinlessness) of his religious (pious) life, and at any stage, that aspect of his life is inseparable from any other aspect, before he enters upon his redemptive work as an adult and during his exercising of it. (3) In our development as humans we are to become not indistinguishably identical to him but, in proper measure *like* him. Only he alone lives perfectly in God's image, and he transmits that image to the rest of humanity, beginning with Christians. (4) Jesus' relationship to God is that of a humble servant and, in that way of a Son to a progenitor Father, as he explores here in unusual detail as in two "forms," this kind of human being, himself growing and increasing and correspondingly as revealing God's gracious activity toward all and in all humanity, hence in his person and teaching.

with beholding the holy, pure, marvelous, and innocent child Jesus. May this divine image purify the love and work that we are dedicating to future generations. May this image permeate us to the effect that we would seek to keep human nature pure from all the world's disorder in those who are given to us. Throughout our lives may we have in mind beholding the way our Redeemer developed and increased in grace, and may we do as in our relation to God and also to all human beings whenever we are in a position to affect one another. May this process that holds before us a sacred image provided by Jesus Christ, though one that we never did attain to, actually be one, to be sure, that in each element of life both contributes to our eliminating false pretense and addends to purifying love! Then this process occurs in and among us in such a way that our minds and hearts might partake of the heavenly light that radiates from him!

Above everything else, however, may beholding his undefiled holiness drive us to do away with every sin that takes hold in us, so that we might purely maintain the divine factor within ourselves, so that the holiness that already radiates toward us from the eyes of the newborn Christ might come to be our own share! May the result also be that within us as well the divine Redeemer might be born in us anew. May this result occur in and among us, so that we too might come to be human beings as he was and become ever more capable of appearing in divine form! To that end, let us give homage to the divine child, the Savior of the world, holding fast to his holy image from the very moment when he first appeared to us, so that it might grow and increase within us, and so that our entire human nature might be formed in likeness to him! May all this occur and flourish in and among us, for the sake of him by whose name we are called Christians, a name that is above all names and before which all knees should bend in heaven and on earth! Amen.

4

That the Redeemer Is Born as the Son of God

Christmas Sermon
December 25, 1821[1]

Glory to God in the Highest and on Earth
Peace to People of Good Will.

And now, you will . . . bear a son, and you will name him Jesus.
He will be great, and will be called the Son of the Most High.

—LUKE 1:31, 32 (NRSV)

These, my devout friends, were the angel's words of promise to Mary: the
son she was to bear will be named a son of the Most High. Moreover, as
subsequently this promise is directly connected with those other words,
that the power of the Most High would overshadow her, Mary had no
cause to think that, as it were, sometime in the future her son was to become the Son of God through some outstanding deeds or by divine grace
pouring over him later on. Rather, she had to think that he would be the
Son of God as soon as she bore him, since from then on she was to call

---

1. This 1821 sermon was thoroughly revised to be read and was originally published in *Festpredigten* (1826), 87–110, then in SW II.2 (1834, 1843), 55–66, and in
other German collections, recently in KGA III.6 (2017) and in an earlier *Selected Sermons of Schleiermacher*, ET: Mary Wilson (1890), 279–94.

him by his name, Jesus. Further, my Christian friends, precisely this is also the complete meaning of our festive Christmas joy today and always. This is so, for if the Redeemer of the world had not been at all different from other human children at his birth, but if the divine that we adore in him had descended upon him from above only later, then our special relationship to him would not begin with his birth. Moreover, in our joy concerning his appearance we would have to adhere not so much to his birth, which would not yet have made him the Redeemer, but rather to that moment in his life when he might have been filled in a special way with the power of the Most High.

Thus, this is the focus for everything that moves our hearts in these festive days: that the Redeemer is already born as the Son of God, that the divine power that put him in a position to redeem the world dwelt within him from the very beginning of his life; and may this be the special subject of our devout reflection for today. Thus, let us see how this focus necessarily coheres, on the one hand, with our shared Christian faith, but also coheres, on the other hand, with the love by which faith has an active component.[2]

2. In the previous year, 1820, Schleiermacher's Christmas sermon had served to introduce his entire theological outlook to his congregation. On this account, I recently translated that sermon and placed it in another book, which appropriately concludes a Mapping the Tradition series at Lexington/Fortress Academic, as its centerpiece: *Schleiermacher: The Psychology of Christian Faith and Life* (2018). In *Schleiermacher's Sermons* (1997) I had accounted for thirty tightly interwoven sermons extant from 1820, which focused especially on the life of Jesus, itself situated at the center of his doctrinal theology (see *Christian Faith* §§11 and 92, ET: Tice et al., 2016). In Winter Term 1819–20 he had lectured on "The Life of Christ" for the first time, followed in 1821 by lectures comparing stories on Jesus' passion in Summer Term 1821. He was to lecture on Jesus' life as a whole again in 1823 and 1829/30, though this first appeared only in SW I.6 (1864; ET: *The Life of Jesus*, Gilmour, 1975). From 1839 to 1863, Hegelian theologian David Friedrich Strauss (1806–1874) severely attacked his views on Christ Jesus, having heard the 1829 lectures, and thoroughly denounced them. To set the record straight, a manuscript of them was included in SWI.6 (1864). Rather late. Too late? Strauss reiterated his critique in the next year in *Der Christus des Glaubens und der Jesus der Geschichte, eine Kritik des Schleiermacherschen Lebens Jesus* (Berlin, 1865). Controversy over the contrast Strauss thus indicated between the historical Jesus and the Christ of faith has continually arisen ever since. Schleiermacher had argued that the two figures would remain largely the same person and initiated a critical examination of the New Testament sources. He had already lectured on what later became *Christian Faith* during his first term at Halle (1804–1807) and four terms at Berlin (1808/09, 1811, 1812/13, 1816); he had also lectured on the *Christian Faith* Introduction (Summer 1818), on the book as a whole (1812, 1818/19); then he spoke on the First Part (1820/21) and then on the Second Part (in 1821 and also during four more terms—ending up with ten hours per week (two hours daily and

I

To be sure, it would be a hard saying if, in the first place, we would assert, my good friends, that it coheres with the core of our Christian faith as expressed on this very festive day, then also to say that we cannot and may not imagine the Redeemer other than as supplied with divine power, already from the initial moment of his appearance in this world. What he offered includes everything that he had to have to be the Redeemer of the world, already bearing within himself the eternal divine Word, even if still silently, and bearing the light that was to shine into the darkness. This would be so even if this light were still concealed, and thereby already bearing what is distinguished by this redeeming power's dwelling within him presumably before all sinners had existed and thereby separated from the human community of sin.

Now, this entire assertion would be a hard saying to be sure, my dear friends, because in spiritual matters—for by way of contrast, in bodily and natural matters we do constantly encounter such—it is difficult to expect that we are to place our trust in something that in its entire nature we cannot vividly and clearly imagine and cannot illuminate to the point of its being a distinct image within ourselves. Yet, this very process is expected of us here. This is so, for suppose that we cannot even deny knowing something about an intimate union of a divine power with the human soul in accordance with its original divine endowment. Such a union is our experience inasmuch as everyone who could boast of belonging to Christ should indeed also know that they have partaken of the Holy Spirit. Moreover, the latter experience would indeed be of a divine nature, because through the divine Spirit we are to become at one with God. In this way, we would then also know that we could not really receive this divine gift in its entirety until human consciousness would already have opened for us in its fullness, and all original spiritual powers would have awakened those human powers over which the Spirit of God is to reign directly and supremely.[3] As a result, the divine Spirit could then also engender this reign, and thus the Spirit's sanctifying activity could

five weekly sessions). After the first edition of *Christian Faith* was published in two volumes (1821–1822), he had students read the results and contributed new items to discussions held during the same ten hours per week thereafter (1823/24, 1825, 1827/28, 1830). Once the second edition had appeared (1830–1831), much revised but with similar content overall, he did not lecture further in this discipline.

3. See *Christian Faith* (2016), Analytical Index on "supernatural become natural."

arise immediately. Moreover, we would also never become conscious of the divine Spirit except through this same sanctifying activity.[4]

Yet, let us imagine that the divine power of the Redeemer would have to be in the Redeemer while he was still in the most incomplete condition in which a human being ever appears to us, namely that of newborn babies, in whom all those powers would still slumber in which the higher divine power in Christ could be revealed and manifested. We would then have to think that this power would be present but without our being able to imagine any efficacious action that it would perform. This result would indeed be difficult for us to imagine. For this reason, moreover, it would also be hard for us to have faith.

Precisely for this reason, at all times in the Christian church there has also been a notion such as I indicated previously. The notion holds that not only in the years of his childhood but also until everything human in him had matured, the Redeemer would have been nothing other than what all other human children are, and would have carried within himself, bearing no features other than what all other human children do. The notion also holds that only when he was to enter the great calling to which he was destined would the power of God have come over him and permeated his entire being. Precisely for this reason it also happens that many other Christians, although not attached to this opinion, could indeed not sincerely join in the childlike devotion that with the complete reverence by which a grateful soul would dedicate itself to the Redeemer, would thereby go back to the first beginning of his life and would recognize the Son of God already in the newborn child. This would presumably occur despite his relative lack of a corresponding unconscious state. As a result, nothing new could be imparted to him from above. Rather,

4. The "divine Spirit" becomes the "Holy Spirit" there. See also his denial of any supposed preexisting entity corresponding to Christ before Jesus' appearance, in *Christian Faith* (2016), §15.2. In this 1821 sermon, Schleiermacher had been critiquing this traditional doctrine, which he tended to supplant by emphasizing the "one eternal divine decree of creation and redemption." See *Christian Faith* (2016), Analytical Index on this subject. In *Christian Faith* (2016), §120.2 he also includes "faith" in relation to election. A major result of election is a process of "sanctification" through a communal life in the divine Spirit's meeting the human spirit, i.e. in and with Christ's God-consciousness, itself a communion of the Son with the Father passed on to the human "children of God." See especially *Christian Faith* (2016), Analytical Index on "sanctification." By this organic interconnection of thematic materials Schleiermacher can explain in this 1821 sermon in what ways Christ was (and was not) preexistent, as some had affirmed (echoing a gnostic interpretation of John 1:1), meaning that "in the beginning" the Word was about sin and grace "with God" and "was God."

through the normal development of a human soul, he would have become the one who by word and deed, by life and death, would earn or bring forth the faith or belief that even these more doubting Christians would also entertain, namely, that he is the Son of the living God, the one through whom in the last days God thus spoke to human beings as a whole for the last time, and after whom we may not expect another. [So, just as God spoke in the Genesis narrative, saying, in effect, "let humans be created," so this speaking is actually what is assumed in the Pauline "new creation."]

Suppose, however, that these co-Christians simply wanted to understand themselves in proper fashion. Suppose that they were simply serious about this faith or belief in the Son of the living God, and in accordance with it also about the communal association that brings us together at this festive occasion. Would they nevertheless not then have to agree with us that it would be at least as difficult to have to give up this faith, or belief, (on which today's celebration is also based, simply because we cannot comprehend the beginning of the second creation any better than we can comprehend the beginning of the first creation—and generally every subsequent beginning? This question arises, for we must also wonder at this: Suppose that the divine Word had not already become flesh when Christ first opened his human eyes; what would further follow from this claim?

This much has gained surety for us, my good friends: Something is to be pointed out that is not only our own experience alone, but we also present it boldly and firmly as the general human experience to which an exception has never been found, nor can one be found. It is the experience that sooner or later sin also develops in all human beings, who from birth onward are equipped only as every human child appearing on earth is equipped. Moreover, any distinction among human beings, however great it may appear to us to be, though basically this difference would always be only slight as to the power of one's understanding and of one's strength of will. Further, however one may regard this difference, it would always effect only a more or less in the development of sin. That this development of sin could ever be lacking in a soul that enters life equipped only in this way, however, would entirely inveigh against the testimony of our consciousness.[5]

---

5. In *Christian Faith* (2016) see the discussions on sin and especially on the sinlessness of the Redeemer. The critical examination of optimal notions in this sermon clearly represents a clarification of those rejected in regard to Jesus' relationship with

Accordingly, we could also not think otherwise than that the same thing would have befallen even the Redeemer, if from birth he would have been like any other human child. It would not matter what promises the angel laid upon the humble soul of Mary, how thoughtfully she might have composed and prepared herself in childlike and heartfelt fear of God for the great task of being the mother and caretaker of him who was to be called the Son of the Most High. Nonetheless, suppose that precisely this latter state were taken to have come to him only in future, this effect, no matter how faithfully and wisely she might have watched over his delicate mind and heart, however far from him she may have kept everything that could have infected him with the widespread poison that all human children at some time or other unfortunately inhale and exhale. Precisely for this reason, she would also not have been able to keep sin from him, for here we recognize the limits of all human love and faithfulness and wisdom, even in the most nearly perfect instances.

Now then, suppose that Christ had remained a sinner even in the smallest degree, could he then be our Redeemer? God could have spoken through him as God did through the prophets of the Old Testament, who were also sinful human beings, but do we want to bear the name of a prophet? Do we want to gather in the name of a prophet whose actions would indeed have been merely a continuation of what was old and would have brought nothing new? Indeed, just as sin cannot be present on a small scale anywhere, or still less can even be conceived on a small scale, so we could also never be sure that this continuation of the old way would be the final one. Suppose, moreover, that what God would have spoken through our Redeemer could have been a more nearly perfect teaching and instruction. In that instance, what he could have done could have been a purer example, but each such example would always be simply one of some law. Moreover, whether a law given externally and engraved on stone or bronze tablets would come down directly from heaven, or whether it would be given by and from a human being, humankind could never be redeemed by such a law. Rather, even if it were spoken by the holiest of mouths or written with the very finger of God, such a law could bring about only a knowledge of sin, and in itself this knowledge would afford no redemption. Instead, the more exactly we would know sin, the

---

his mother, Mary. Remarks made in this sermon seem to be consistent with those made in *Christian Faith* regarding the life and efficacious action of Jesus, Christ, and Redeemer, in *Christian Faith* (2016); though Mariology is somewhat included therein, no sinless perfection is attributed to her.

more would we simply be moved to call out: Who will redeem me from the body of death?[6] Instead, redemption would have to consist precisely in sin's being extinguished from our very consciousness. Thus, sinlessness would have to step before our very eyes, and this living sinlessness is indeed characteristic of the Redeemer himself. Moreover, only by our appropriating this vision in most intimate affinity and union with him, as everything he brings is held in common among all who are thereby befriended, can we partake of the peace and blessedness that are the fruits of redemption.

Now, could this sinlessness in him have appeared to us and have enjoined us to such devotion if later, in some mysterious fashion, the Redeemer would have been filled with the divine Spirit and divine power, even if this accomplishment were to have been without restriction and performed in a way not at all to be compared with what those Old Testament prophets did? After sustaining this change, would he still be and remain a human being and indeed the same human being, and not take on a mere spectral appearance? However venerable this specter might be in its nature, would it not always repel us from itself by its history? If all this were so, then the memory of his earlier life and condition could not be extinguished, even supposing that he could also not have committed any sin after his wondrous sanctification. Yet, if the memory of an earlier sinful condition had remained in him, let us again look at our own experience together with the most general human experience in order to see what more might emerge from this examination.

If we were to do this, we would feel what would follow, my good friends: It would be a saddening experience and one that in many respects we would prefer to conceal and hide rather than to communicate that even the most distant memory of earlier sin that would linger in our soul never lingers therein only as a dead letter, as mere information, as of things past that are now external to us. Rather, this memory would continue to be something alive and not infrequently to defile even our holiest thoughts and deeds, in the initial origin of which we would also have been most distinctly conscious of the power of the divine Spirit. That Spirit would continue to live in and among us to show us that so long as a human being wanders on earth as a sinful human being, however richly the grace of God may pour over a given person, one's soul would never

6. Rom 7:24.

become such a perfectly pure mirror as it could be if something of this poison had never penetrated into its innermost being.

Thus, if the Redeemer had shared this poison with us, he would also have had to undergo this experience as we have done. Moreover, my good friends, do we not know that individually each sin of which only a faint stirring would still have lingered in our souls at some time and in some way—just as some dominant sin does on a larger scale—such a sin would also work in a darkening manner on our understanding, would blind and falsify our judgment, would darken and contaminate our glance into the divine will?

Now, suppose that even our Redeemer would have retained such a fleeting shadow of sin within his soul. How could we then hope of him that the words in which he has proclaimed to us the will of his and our Father in heaven and has presented to us our entire relationship to the Father, would be of so perfect a truth and would be based on such a pure and complete comprehension that humankind could always remain directed to it? How could we assume that a perfect harmony existed in him, that everything that is flesh in him was wholly permeated by the divine Spirit and became one with that Spirit? How could we then infer that as a result he would indeed be the example that everyone was meant to imitate, the leader in whose footsteps everyone was to step, this without our being able to hope ever to exhaust his truth, even through the most self-disciplined appropriation of it, or to hope ever to attain to his example, even by our most faithful obedience? Moreover, we would indeed have needed such a Redeemer had we found ourselves completely satisfied, retaining no wish that yet another might come after him!

Now, my dear friends, let us add to all this the great and important words that the Redeemer himself used to describe what so essentially distinguishes him from all sons and daughters of the earth when he says in his conversations: I and the Father are one; who sees me sees the Father. Let us consider that, at the same time, these words contain the standard for our union with the Redeemer himself as it is given to us in faith but is to be reached in reality only ever more nearly perfectly, as he prayed for us that we too would come to be at one with him. Based on this consideration, it already follows of itself that whoever sees us also sees him! How could we take these words spoken by him in any way other than in their full and complete sense as they lie before us? Moreover, how could the Redeemer have spoken such words without appearing to us on their account as one who either deceives himself or (even if well-intentioned, so that enough would be accepted) requires stronger expressions than would accord with truth and so would deceive those who would want to take these same words exactly but with the result of their retaining vain hopes?

To be sure, he would have to appear this way to us if he had spoken in this manner and thereby had also tasted sin, even if only from a distance. This is so, for how could a person in whom only the faintest trace of sin remained say that he is one with the Father—the Father of light, the Father who is alone good and pure and whom all persons also approach only to the degree that each one participates in what is good and pure? Thus, if he spoke honestly and if there is a communion between him and us such that it is an effusion of the union between him and the Father, then already from the beginning of his life he must have borne within himself the Word of God that must have protected him from everything that resembles sin, even if only from afar. Then, this Word of God must have watched over each development of his natural human powers in such a way that even what was sense oriented remained pure and, as it were, both waited confidently for a gradual entrance of a noticeable efficacy derived from this indwelling divine power and, from the beginning onward, also strove to be nothing other than an instrument for that power. Only if he were like this from the very beginning of his life could he rightly say this of himself.

Finally, my good friends, let us also think once again on the holiness of the one before whom, precisely because of sin, people wholly lacked the glory that we were to enjoy in connection with him, and let us consider that we thus needed such a helper for the sake of whom this holy God could deem and declare the entirety of humankind to be eventually pure and who would represent us all with his Father because of his own perfect purity. Oh, in God's holy sight not even the slightest trace of corruption and of sin would remain hidden! Suppose that before God something, even if only in the smallest portion, a tiny portion that might well elude any other eye, should appear impure. Then, everything would have to be considered impure! Thus, my good friends, let us consider the role of our inner faith, given our advocacy of our Redeemer's union with the Father, our belief that in him we see the image of the heavenly Father and the reflection of the Father's splendor, our belief in the unsurpassability and the constant continuation of the Redeemer's teaching as well as in the sufficiency and irrefutability of his commandments. All of this would then depend on the fact that he has already appeared in this world as the eternal Word that became flesh, as the light from above that shone into the darkness.

II

However, let us now see, in the second place, that if we do not think of the Redeemer in this way, as pure and unvarnished love, then the source of this love, which is the Redeemer himself, would be lacking its proper grounding. This would be the case, on the one hand, in that there would exist no unvarnished purity of true Christian love, but also, on the other hand, its extension over the entirety of humankind would actually rest on the fact that he, for the sake of whom we thus love and without reference to whom there would be no striving after such a love at all, is such a Redeemer as is described for us in our text.

My good friends, unquestionably one of the most striking phenomena in the human soul is the struggle between the love that we all bear for those who are like us and the pure feeling we have regarding right and wrong, regarding good and evil. Both sides of this contrast, equally very much grounded in the most noble aspect of our nature, nonetheless do constantly work against each other. No matter how firm we may be in our displeasure with and resistance to a given wrong, if we find it in a person who already has gripped our heart in love, how inclined we would be then to excuse and to see even what is most hated in a softer light. Suppose that we are viewing a human figure and that this human being is drawing us to itself with love. Suppose too that we are noticing the stirring of sin there, that we are observing outbursts of sensory corruption and foolish delusion there. Then one's soul, the more it is devoted to truth and to what is good, would be all the more gripped by a displeasure that would only too easily change into passion and that would suppress love.[7]

If we found ourselves wandering among only those like ourselves, if we found no love objects except companions as corrupt as we are, then would we be capable of a clear, unclouded love, or would we be capable only of a love that would repeatedly obscure our noblest feelings? Could we wish simply that our moral feeling might become incapable

---

7. The theme of humans' bearing love for one another in response to God's love as expressed in the Redeemer's influence upon us is an almost constant theme among the Christmas sermons. However, this theme too is freshly analyzed here. See items under "love" in indexes to his *Christmas Eve Celebration* (ET: Tice, 2011) and *Christian Faith* (2016).

of expressing vehement emotions—of those emotions we might offer harshly, cuttingly, or with an undertone of enmity (whether in judgment or in active resistance) when we supposedly confront people we love? No, suppose that we could not give up our noble and powerful anger toward everything contrary to the divine will! Hence, we could also not avoid doing anything but loving ourselves just as little as we love our brothers and sisters, for even the necessary and unexceptionable love we each have for ourselves would be stained in the same manner. Moreover, the more stern a given person might be in this respect, the more loud may be the inward divine voice speaking within any one of us, and the more often might we find each one in transition and change between an undisturbed enjoyment of pleasure in some fortunate progress of which one is aware, and the most noble self-contempt.

Furthermore, it could indeed not be demanded more firmly, or even in a different sense and in a different manner, that each of us is to love our neighbor as ourselves. So, consider the case of anyone who loves oneself only in this very manner, and who, at the same time, is always equally severe toward oneself. There could be few individuals—even among those who are most highly esteemed, also who generally appear to be the best and most noble in respect to whom judgment and sensibility should not switch between self and others in the same way, or as might occur concerning themselves. There could be only a few such individuals, provided that some one individual would be connected with one's inner self in relation to other individuals such that the connection could be so close that their innermost being would be almost perfectly clear to oneself. In this case, the attendant grief would then be quite general! This would be so, for surely we have to sense that over each instance of human love a darker shadow rests, by which a pure light is dimmed and is split into fragmented rays, so that the blessedness of love is thwarted for us.

Yet, as Christians must we not reject this condition? Is it not unvarnished love to which Scripture summons us? Could the Lord's disciples be recognized by the love they shared among themselves if this love had been distinguished only in an indefinite way, by something more or something less than this natural yet unfortunately so unsatisfactory love—a love still found among all supposedly uncorrupted human beings? Well! The question arises: How would we then be able to attain to another love for others and thus also for ourselves?

Indeed, suppose that Christ were such an uncorrupted person, if in him we would recognize the divine being so originally united with human nature that in our love for him each of the two loves mentioned would be one in the fullest way possible—that is, we are speaking about our love for those like us, and love for the will of the heavenly Father. Then we would have at least one human being to whom we could be devoted with completely pure and unvarnished love, just as his love for us could also be completely pure and unvarnished. This would be the case, for it could not cause disruption in his love for us that he would not find in us this other life, this splendor of the divine will. Rather, finding such lacks in us could impress only the distinctive mark of helpful empathy upon what he finds. Moreover, we, remembering the heavenly voice—"This is my beloved Son, in whom I am well pleased"[8]—would live in firm trust that if in faith we can say simply and with genuine truth, "Not I but Christ lives in me,"[9] then God too would see us not for ourselves alone but only in this communion with Christ that we have, and thus we would also participate in the good pleasure that God finds in God's Son. Precisely by virtue of this faith the circle of our pure and unvarnished love would also necessarily be expanded and would spread over everyone whom we see to be in communion with Christ.[10] Consequently, what we still find of human corruption in our brothers and sisters would also seem to us to be removed and extinguished already by the effecacious participation of Christ in them, and this observation could only arouse us with the same love with which he has loved us—this for the purpose of furthering the life of Christ in them. Thereby that life would become even fuller and would totally overcome the sin that, as a surely passing phenomenon, would simply be there in memory, to remind us that the blessedness we find in unvarnished love is a gift that we have received from above, and also to remind us that all of this could arise for us only because of the one human being, Christ.[11]

See, this is a love different from the natural love that we examined. We can say, "The old is past; behold, everything has become new."[12] Yet,

8. Matt 3:17 (NRSV).

9. Gal 2:20 (NRSV).

10. Both "communion" and "community" translate *Gemeinschaft* in such doctrinal contexts as this one. See *Christian Faith* (2016), Analytical Index for examples.

11. On other of Schleiermacher's treatments of traditional doctrines on this subject see *Christian Faith* (2016), Analytical Index, "Christ, two-natures of." This part of the sermon adds a fresh slant to the many passages therein that analyze his alternative view.

12. 1 Cor 5:17 (NRSV).

we can love in this way only through him and for his sake. That cloudy, imperfect natural love cannot, as it were, be cleansed to the point of purity on its own. That one human being who directly requires and awakens pure love had to be given to us. Only in this way could what is imperfect draw perfection into itself. Only in this way could our love for others be sanctified aright, in cases when it would be nothing but an outflowing of our natural love for him and a reflection of his merely natural love for us.

In contrast, suppose, first, that he were not one such that only pure love, without the slightest hint of imperfection in him, who is himself beloved, and suppose that this pure love were alone in accord with the impression that he would make on us. If our impression had been that the name Christ is not of one who loves purely, then we would always have remained in the old, imperfect state, and nothing better would be allotted to us. This would be so, for suppose that, as we just explained, it were true that something sinful would ever stir in Christ during his human life, and so that even he would not be in a position to blot out the memory of that sin and its living traces within himself. How much, then, would we want to restrain ourselves from sinning and prevent our own sins—however magnificently he might have appeared to us in his later, mature public life, in his sacred proclamation of God's reign, in the courage and certainty with which he invited human beings to come to himself and promised them comfort and peace. Indeed, he appeared in order to exercise all these roles as the most excellent among all human beings, as the most highly chosen and greatest instrument of God. How would we then want to restrain ourselves nonetheless and, preventing our eyes from being pained in our searching out the traces of sin within ourselves, if we knew that those traces of sin would have to exist in him? Indeed, the less we would succeed in locating particular, definite imperfections and deficiencies anywhere in Christ's life, the more surely would we presuppose that concealed deficiencies would nevertheless be contained in all that was glorious in his life that we are accustomed especially to praise and extol in him. Whether we would always simply have to presuppose them or would actually have discovered them severally, would be a matter of indifference for love. We might be able to love him infinitely much more than everyone else; and we might be able to adhere to him with a reverence to which no other relation to him could be compared. However, this would also be an impure, varnished love, nevertheless. It would not be different from the love that we offer to other human beings. Thus, even his own love could not serve to sanctify and transform.

Second, however, true Christian love would also necessarily cohere with this notion of the Redeemer inasmuch as this love is to be a totally universal love and just as his redemptive work is to embrace the entirety of humankind. That is, generally we do actually view this love as an impetus within human nature that is totally independent of Christ's appearance, and we actually consider it to be a command emerging from human reason that wherever we see human beings we are also to enter immediately into the relationship of giving and of receiving love. However, we simply do not always remember that even this love first came to us through Christ and that it is one of the sad and devastating consequences of sin that it constricts and restricts love within the human heart. Before the Son of God appeared, where then were the people, where does history refer us to the human beings, who, indeed, I do not want to say would truly have felt and practiced but would simply have required of themselves and others a general and unlimited love? In individual souls devoted to quiet reflection, such a notion could scarcely be developed—such a notion would die away without having become a vital impetus somewhere, and even in these souls this notion would not have been preserved more strongly whenever they would have returned to active life. This would be so, for was not love limited everywhere to those who shared a common language and origin, so that to each person everything human outside these limits appeared to be if not inimical then a matter of indifference? Further, truly that love was also completely natural, for precisely the same reason mentioned earlier: There would have been a reason that could require a universal connection for love, and that could also proclaim both that it would have been endemic throughout humankind and that in each of the larger parts of humanity inequalities of all sorts would also have been endemic, by virtue of which some people could give more and others would have to receive more. Each individual, however, could receive more easily from someone who spoke one's own language than from others, and each individual could also share more easily with one's own than with others. Thus, in this way it would have seemed appropriate that each individual would continue to stick with one's own, and, based on this separation, strife and hate would also have developed as often as the separated areas got entangled by the fault of individuals or by the urgency of human needs. Moreover, experience teaches us that we would not have been freed from this restriction of love. This we have learned, because it is still like this everywhere to the degree that human hearts have not yet perfectly paid homage to the one shepherd of the one flock. We would not have been freed from this restriction by means of any or all human wisdom that could have appeared somewhere, by means of each moderation of customs that might have emerged over the course of time.

Suppose, however, that this opinion were to cease, namely the opinion that each individual could find in oneself what is needed and what brings blessing, or salvation, because everywhere one can look, everything is indeed imperfect, but, at the same time, some seed of what is good and true does also exist. Suppose a rumor were then to have arisen that in one place a stream of light from on high should appear, a pure light that could and would dispel all darkness. Suppose further that, on the one hand, the hearts of certain people should turn toward this light due to their being fed up with what was imperfect but, on the other hand, that the Redeemer, being one with the Father in the selfsame love for the entirety of humankind, had come to them, and, holding faith that he was the Son of the living God, they would have instilled confidence in those who held faith in him. That is, if they brought him and his peace to people, they would give them something not to be obtained in any other way anywhere. Moreover, the love of Christ would compel them to spread their proclamation farther and ever farther. Then, the walls of partition could fall and a universality of love could be poured into people's hearts, a love that itself gleams through the unfortunately still continuing strife of earthly life and that overcomes it ever more from within outward.[13]

Yet, where would that limiting and separating spirit of a people be any sharper or more severe than where our Lord was actually born? This was a people who considered all other peoples impure and avoided their company, among whom, viewed as an interpretation of a divine Word, the teaching was promulgated: "You are to love your brethren and hate your enemy." This was a people who did not at all recognize the determination that they were to be held together under such a constricting law only until the light of the world would appear. Moreover, due to a misunderstanding of this law, they imagined that this very law was God's own law. Such a people could not of itself alone beget, care for, and instruct the Redeemer, from whom this love for each and all was to proceed. If

---

13. The process described here, as earlier in this 1821 sermon, is "broadening action" in and on behalf of the church, the final one of three that were to be featured in his 1822/23 companion lectures on Christian Ethics, ed. by Ludwig Jonas (SWI.12; partial ET: Brandt, *Selections* [2011]). The other main headings are "presentational action" and "purifying [or reforming] action."

the divine Word had not dwelt within him from the very beginning,[14] protecting and guarding him, how could he have escaped this ancient limitation, which was rooted in the entire life of this people and was made sacred by their entire historical tradition? Or are we to believe that he too had not escaped this limitation and that only his disciples would have got beyond it? Would his disciples have done this—his disciples, who had everything only from him but so often had not understood even what he wanted to share with them; his disciples, who, even after he had gone, spoke and acted only from the divine Spirit he had fostered, which could and was to do nothing but simply take the divine Word from Christ and illuminate it for them! Surely we cannot believe this, for no disciple had climbed above the master, and almost only in resistance were they carried away into community with the Samaritans and with Gentiles by the Lord's command to "proclaim the gospel among all peoples." In contrast, he was securely placed over and against all influences of this limiting mode of thinking by the divine Word that he bore within himself from the very outset. By virtue of his oneness with the Father, he was the originator of a universal love. Moreover, the universal union of all human beings that was founded by him and that was eternally oriented to the humanization to be found in his person, this universal union was composed of the same divine power that holds all things together.[15]

Further, my good friends, without the faith that we have presented now in brief outline, without that love the image of which we have cursorily sketched out for ourselves, what would then be the value of redemption for us? Where would our blessing, or salvation, be, and where would the righteousness be that Christ was to be and has become for us?

Thus, my good friends, suppose that through him God in heaven is to be honored, and through him the spiritually creative power of the universal Creator is to be glorified—the Creator who has not called the human race simply to its original imperfect condition. Suppose too that through him peace on earth is to be established, the peace before which all discord and hate vanish evermore, in such a way that everything may become one in love. Suppose that a serene good pleasure is to be made

14. John 1:1.

15. Schleiermacher's view of human beings' "embeddedness" and responsibility for care of and respect for creation has grounded what has been shown to be an ecotheology, though he did not literally identify it as such. See Poe, *Essential Trinitarianism* (2017); and Poe, ed., *Schleiermacher and Sustainability* (2018), her edition of a work with other colleagues that displays this grounding.

possible for us, without which, to be sure, no blessedness, or salvation, can be imagined. Then, there has to be a truly divine figure of a Redeemer on whom our eye can rest. Then, from the beginning of his life onward, it has to have been true that the divine Word became flesh in him. Moreover, we have a sacred right to greet him with holy reverence at his appearance on earth, in the first childlike form of human life, to greet him as the one who not only was to become the Redeemer of humankind but was this Redeemer already at his birth. We have the sacred right to greet him not only as the one in whom the Father was to be glorified but as the one in whom he was already glorified invisibly and as the one who was himself one with the Father already from the very beginning.[16]

Yes, my good friends, for all of us this celebration of the Redeemer's childhood is, at the same time, the beautiful and joyous celebration of children, on whom rests our affectionate gaze, with good pleasure precisely in relation to him who also for the children's sake took on flesh and blood such as they themselves possess. Further, the glint in our eye lovingly promises them blessedness, which they will find in their faith in the Redeemer and in their trust in him. So, let us hold firm to the fact that it is only through this faith that otherwise he was indeed a child like other children, but, because he was to be like us in every respect except sin, the divine power by which he could become the Redeemer of the world had to have been efficacious and active in him, even if hidden, already from the very beginning. Let us hold firm to the assurance that only with this faith can the Word that he expressed, having turned toward the younger generation with a loving heart, reach its great fulfillment: Of such is the reign of God.

⚘

Editor's Postscript

All the sermons that follow the Christmas sermons of 1820–1821, over the last fourteen years of Schleiermacher's life, may be viewed either as introducing his mature doctrinal system (set forth in those two years and

---

16. In effect, this paragraph has provided an exegetical interpretation of John 1:1–18. The further reference to children in the concluding paragraph extends this interpretation to the main thesis presented in this sermon regarding what the Redeemer's birth signifies.

then greatly revised in 1830–1831) or as adding thematic explanations to that system. At first, then, they would also serve either to anticipate major theses in the second and final edition of *Christian Faith* (1830–1831)—especially in relation to the chronologically developing core of that doctrinal system—or to present further thematic explanations of these theses. Hence, the sermons after 1821 also reveal certain developments in the doctrinal system and in his tightly corresponding Christian ethics. At present, only the 1822/23 and 1826/27 versions of his *Christian Ethics* manuscripts are available in German; in English translation only excerpts and outlines from the two sets are available, successively—from the 1822/23 lectures a partial translation by James M. Brandt (2011) and in a bilingual set of essays by Hermann Peiter (2010, ed. Tice) and in John C. Shelley's translation of the *Introduction* with his own introduction and notes (1989). Full transcripts from Peiter's German editions, containing detailed comparison of hearers' full transcriptions of the 1826/27 lectures composes volume 1 (2011). Volume 2 is to contain Schleiermacher's own references. This investment, later further carried out by Peiter (1935–), has consisted in a monumental set of Schleiermacher studies from this period, including Schleiermacher's *Christian Ethics* (1826–1827), volume 1, in German (2011) and a bilingual edition of essays on this subject (in German and English; see volume edited by Tice [2010]).[17] Alongside investments in childrearing and the battle over the king's liturgical agenda, it would alone explain the relative paucity of published sermons from the years 1827–1828. The rest of the 1820s shows ample evidence of public remains from Schleiermacher's other activities.

As some would say, "family comes first." In effect, this would be true for Schleiermacher's own family. See his 1818 sermons, revised for publication in 1820 and 1826.[18] By Christmas Day 1820, for which the translated sermon has been featured in another book,[19] Schleiermacher's household was composed of his own three daughters (ages three through ten), a stepdaughter (age fifteen) and a stepson (age thirteen), and of his wife, Henriette (1788–1840). She was twenty years his junior; thus in 1820 she was thirty-two, and she was twenty on their wedding day (in 1809). She was born von Mühlenfels, and she brought the two older children from a short-lived marriage to his close friend, army chaplain Ehrenfried von Willich (1773–1807), who had died of typhoid in 1807.

17. Peiter, *Christliche Ethik bei Schleiermacher* (2010).

18. Schleiermacher, *The Christian Household* (1820); ET: Seidel and Tice, (1991).

19. Tice, *Schleiermacher: The Psychology of Christian Faith and Life* (2018).

In 1820 Henriette gave birth to Schleiermacher's only son, Nathanael Hermann (1820–1829), a bright, vigorous child in whose rearing and education he was at least as loving, intentional, and persistent as was true with all his other five children, including the stepdaughter and stepson brought to the marriage by his wife, and three daughters born of that marriage. Nathanael rapidly died of cholera at age nine. A father's funeral service remarks and a talk at his son's grave have counted as significant testimonies ever since.[20]

Also fulfilled in his household were two common sayings Schleiermacher used widely: "My home is always your home too," and "Our home is yours to be a member of whenever you might need or have a desire for it." His sister Charlotte (Lotte), also an ordered sister among the Herrnhutter Brethren community, had longer and shorter stays in the household over the years. In this period, so did the widow Frau Karoline Fischer, a companion of and helper for Frau Henriette, with her own half-grown daughter, Luise. Following shared principles, members of the Schleiermacher household never had servants and so did not have to prepare and support any servants who wanted to attain a free and independent life and livelihood after a specified time, although Schleiermacher recommended doing just this in what are called his household sermons (1818).[21] In addition, the spouses shared responsibility for one more customary arrangement whereby the wife was honored for handling specific household tasks, and the husband was honored for doing tasks outside the home.

Other work, as it were, beside family and vocational obligations followed the turbulent decades of the 1820s into the equally paced final years of Schleiermacher's life. Works not yet mentioned include a few early sets of Sunday sermons on New Testament books, his *Oratio* (an address on the three-hundredth anniversary of the Reformation), and nine sermons in celebration of the handing over of the Ausburg Confession (1830).[22]

---

20. See Albert L. Blackwell (1977). These documents figured large within liberal progressive educational literature of the nineteenth century, viewed as among Schleiermacher's contributions to such theory.

21. Published in German (1820); ET: Seidel and Tice, *The Christian Household*, (1991).

22. See Schleiermacher, *Handing Over of Augsburg Confession*, (1820); ET: Nichol, (1997).

5

For What Purpose God Has Loved the World in Sending God's Only Begotten Son

Christmas Day
December 25, 1823[1]

Glory to God in the Highest and on Earth
Peace to People of Good Will.

For God so loved the world that he gave his only Son, so that everyone who believes in him may not perish but may have eternal life.

Indeed, God did not send the Son into the world to condemn the world, but in order that the world might be saved through him. Those who believe in him are not condemned; but those who do not believe are condemned already, because they have not believed in the name of the only Son of God.

—JOHN 3:16–18 (NRSV)

---

1. Among seventy-four expository homilies on the Gospel of John in 1823–1826, this untitled one was also published in 1837, edited by Adolph Sydow from "almost word-perfect" transcripts in SW II.8 (1837), 185–96. For further information, see Tice, *Schleiermacher's Sermons* (1997), 76–77; also Kelsey, *Schleiermacher's Preaching* (2007).

My devout friends, we cannot celebrate today's festival more worthily than precisely with these words, in which our Redeemer gives such a splendid testimony regarding himself. This is so, for suppose that we are indeed accustomed—indeed are directed by today's very celebratory event itself—to visualize him, quite especially in these days, in the form of the newborn human child. In that child, to be sure, the fullness of divinity indwelled, but still present invisibly and concealed. In that child, moreover, everything was first to engage for his human appearance, everything by which he was destined to effectuate what he says of himself here. In this way, then, precisely each celebration of his first appearance on earth would be simply an imperfect and inadequate event. It would be all the more so, if we, in that we are remembering his first coming into the world, would not, at the same time, be envisaging the great purpose of his sending. Moreover, as he himself presents this purpose to the one who had come to hear him as a teacher sent by God, let us then consider this more closely with one another, being guided by our text. The first thing, however, that the Redeemer says about himself here is that he appeared to us as a sign of God's love, and—for, to be sure, this purpose is indeed entirely clear in the words "for God so loved the world"—this sign is viewed as the greatest sign that the Creator and Father of the human race could give to it.

What, my good friends, is a sign of divine love for a receptive human mind and heart that has not completely strayed from one's proper path? Quite especially in this moment and certainly in these days too, we all think of the children whom God has given us and lets grow up among us, with whom we are accustomed to celebrate this beautiful and splendid festival in such a very excellent way. Yes, for all of us, each one without exception, these children are a sign of divine love, a sign that God still reigns with God's inspiriting and renewing Spirit over the human race, that, by still letting a rational soul develop anew among us, God's loving purpose with the human race is yet to endure ever longer. Moreover, even if not everyone contributes to the fulfillment of this purpose in the same degree, we do indeed know that it is the course of nature and the order of life that among any sizeable number of people there are always some individuals through whom God is proclaimed and is glorified in some particular manner. Just as in this manner the author of the Letter to the Hebrews compares the Lord with the prophets through whom in times past God spoke to the fathers,[2] so we too may compare the Lord with all

2. Heb 1:1.

those in whom God displays some particular blessing to some part of the human race, even if this part be ever so small. Each such individual is a remarkable and special sign of God's love. However, how far above everyone is the Lord, whose coming among humankind we celebrate now! The Lord is above everyone inasmuch as he, as the only-begotten Son of God in whom we know the most excellent blessing of God, is above all those who simply by adhering to and being united with him have received the power to be God's children, and the Lord is above us all inasmuch as the blessing, or salvation, which he came to show humankind, is itself above everything that any other person can accomplish for one's brothers and sisters in the world. What is the result? The result is that although these characteristics compose something consummately great and significant, they can and must be only a small part of the Lord's own work among human beings.

Moreover, suppose, my good friends, that we celebrate this festival of the Lord's coming in these days not, as it were, based on special tidings that it is precisely at this time of year when the Lord appeared on earth but perhaps in a more natural way. That is, this way is more natural, because this is the very time when the warming and animating sun, after it had distanced itself ever farther from us, again gradually turns closer to us and at this time climbs up ever higher in the heavens to bring a fairer, more joyful element into our lives. Then, so too by his coming the Lord is seen to be the highest image of divine grace, which, to be sure, was never left without some testimony within humankind, though from time to time nevertheless somehow disappeared before the very eyes of a mortal human being, because all earlier signs of love that were held by them but that God had given to human beings had gradually waned. Further, precisely since, as we may say, the abandonment of God by human beings, their distance from God, and their lack of surety about God had reached their own highest point, the Lord appeared to bring back life and light, the blessing of faith and of love, acquaintance with God, indeed the indwelling of God, in human beings by God's Spirit.

Wherever we may look, at what is natural or at what is spiritual, into the past or into the present, indeed even into the future, our Lord remains the supreme sign of divine love, and God could not give human beings a greater sign than that God sent God's only-begotten Son. God sent him, however, as the Lord himself further says in the words of our text, as the subject of faith. God sent him in order that everyone who has faith or believe in him would not perish but would have eternal life.

What, my good friends, is this great, mysterious power of faith, and yet, on the other hand, we may ask, in turn, what is this so obvious power of faith? It is indeed precisely that of a human soul's faith in the Lord as its Redeemer. It is something, to be sure, that only those individuals know (though one need not say it) who know how to celebrate in the proper manner (that is, in the depths of their minds and hearts, full of modesty and gratitude) this festival and every other festival of the Lord. Moreover, we probably cannot explain this matter to others who do not yet feel within themselves precisely this power of faith. However, in the brief words that he says to Nicodemus, the Lord himself gives us an indication of faith's power (a power we can hold precisely and can realize vividly) when he says: "As Moses lifted up the serpent in the wilderness, even so must the Son of Man be lifted up."[3] It was also a power of faith that by which those who were bitten by poisonous serpents had to look up at the serpent raised before them in order to be healed from what would otherwise have brought death to them. Precisely this looking up and this being healed by looking up, my good friends, is a wonderful symbol of the power of faith, a symbol that expresses this better and more comprehensively than any other merely human wisdom could have done.[4]

---

3. John 3:14 (NRSV).

4. Already in the 1791 sermon above (published in 1801) Schleiermacher uses the ambiguity of *Glaube* (the German word for both internally derived and held "faith" and then externally expressed and publicly codified "belief"). Thus, here too one's inner faith is placed in its psychological connection with feeling and perception, also with both "love" and "wisdom." Each of these pairs of functioning contains that same ambiguity, only one that is clearly differentiated as to level and type of mental fine-tuning. That is, in relation to God in Christ, inner "faith" (immediately held in "feeling" and, at the same time, in "perception") is then cognitively *expressed*, as a "mode of knowing," even of having knowledge, carried in one's "belief." Here is another once-ambiguous category that had entered into Schleiermacher's project of forming a German vocabulary that could convey more exactly distinguishable mental functions. The word *Sinn*, for example could then indicate a great many mental functions and still does, referring to everything from the senses to productions of intellect and thereby to meanings. Other words made from *Sinn* as their root were—and still could be—ambiguous words that Schleiermacher made into much more exact terms for regular scientific use. For example, *Sinnlichkeit* could mean "sensuality," "sensitivity," (of one or more of the senses) or "sensibility." In *On Religion* and *Soliloquies*, *Sinn* itself could be restricted to the third meaning: "sensibility." Well before 1823, *Gesinnung* had also been selected for the exact meaning of "disposition." Here it is to stand for benevolence and love, or wisdom. Occasionally, preferences for selections like these are to be found in Adelung's Dictionary, in use during this period. Such selections were already clearly in evidence when Schleiermacher began lecture courses on Psychology in 1819.

What, my good friends, can we do other than simply look up to the Redeemer, for he always remains above us in an unattainable fashion. If he directly considers us worthy of being called his brothers and sisters,[5] if we directly realize and accept that with thankful hearts, then indeed we must admit that we cannot place ourselves directly at his level. God's children and the only Son of God are not and cannot be on an equal standing. Moreover, what may we do other than to return precisely at the consciousness of what poisoned the existence of each one of us without exception, at the consciousness of sin, in order to feel that we can always merely look up at the one who was acquainted with no sin in himself? However, if those who are looking up are then healed from the poison by looking up, what can we imagine thereby other than a mysterious power that precisely by that source was spread over to those brothers and sisters and flowed into them.

So, my good friends, suppose that it is also nothing other than the process of looking up at the Redeemer to which the mysterious power of his redemption is connected. Suppose too that we look up to him like those who were bitten, conscious of what defiles our nature and ever again threatens to kill our spiritual life, because the Word of promise is that we are to be healed by him.[6] Then, the mysterious power that God placed in him pours into our souls, and at that point the one at whom we look up descends, as it were, to us. Further, precisely by a mysterious power pouring into us from him, by our becoming one with him in the living community of faith in him and, as he himself promised, by his being united with us as the Father was with him,[7] thereby the work for the sake of which he came is indeed accomplished.

We must ask, however, how were we not to believe that one or more among those bitten by serpents considered at least making an effort to look up worthwhile, even without firm faith and irrefutable confidence? Ah, my good friends, thereby how should that word of a likewise needy soul not come to mind, the soul that said to the Lord: "Lord, I believe; help my unbelief"?[8] This is to say, for since everything in the human soul does grow and develop toward being a proper power only gradually, how

5. Luke 8:21.

6. Isa 53:5.

7. John 17:22, 23. In Schleiermacher's sense the words "one," "at one," and "united with" cannot be taken to mean "identical with," "exactly the same thing as," or "simply a part of" in relationship to God *in se*.

8. Mark 9:24 (NRSV).

could it be otherwise than that faith in the Lord also has to be imperfect initially and not yet have come to full strength in the soul when it looks up to him for the first time? Suppose, however, that what is also required is simply this first beginning. Then, what first gives all faith surety is added, namely, experience. We do not have this experience in the way or in such a short period of time as those who noted soon after looking up at the bronze serpent that the poison had lost its power in the body. Rather, we come to have it throughout our entire life, and by this experience faith must be ever strengthened.[9]

How great the healing is that falls upon the human soul by our Lord! This he says, however, as he continues: All who have faith, or believe, in him do not perish but have eternal life. Moreover, elsewhere he also says more than once, "One who has faith, or believes, in me has eternal life."[10] Immediately thereafter he also says, "For the Son of God is sent into the world not to judge the world but to save the world."[11] Eternal life and blessing, or salvation: It is this for which the Son of God was sent into the world, to bring all of this to human beings and, indeed, to bring it, not only as a distant hope, as it were, but as a present good.

In order to have perished and to have eternal life the Redeemer contrasts the assertion that here, without distinguishing and determining to what end someone who does not yet partake of eternal life would simply perish and/or would simply have perished. We all know and feel this very thing, my good friends: Namely, that the path to life and to blessedness is simple, whereas the paths of corruption are manifold. A human being can perish in relation to this or that factor, whereas one finds eternal life only with and by means of one person. Ah, a thousand voices, moreover, attest to us how, without the coming of the Lord into the world, human beings could have perished and would have remained perished, going astray, each one in one's own way.[12] To be sure, for us these conditions should all sound merely remote, precisely because we live in

---

9. Here "experience" (*Erfahrung*—having gone through a process in life) is seen, doctrinally accounted for, as having gone through a process of conversion, most likely an extended process, thence to be released beyond justification (including a stirring of faith by divine grace) into a sure process of sanctification in faith one's whole life long. All this can happen despite setbacks of any sort, so that one is never to be rejected by God in Christ thereafter, presumably not even after one's death.

10. John 3:16; see also John 5:24 (NRSV).

11. John 3:17 (NRSV).

12. Isa 53:6.

the enjoyment of and in possession of all the goods that the Lord has gained for us. However, if we were simply to listen correctly, we would find all these voices within us, precisely because we do not experience whole and perfect sanctification of the soul by faith in one element alone. What poisons human nature and brings corruption to it grows gradually. The attentive eye finds traces of it everywhere within oneself. The poisoning agent wants to reemerge now here, now there, and it wants to spoil whatever joyfulness exists within our hearts. Without exception, moreover, we all perish in corruption by means of everything that distances us from that one person in whom we have faith, or believe, and whom we love. However, what becomes of the person who clings to faith, who does not retreat from union with that one other person in whom God revealed Godself to human nature? This person, my good friends, will not perish, whatever dangers may threaten him or her. This person, my good friends, will not perish, whatever dangers may threaten him or her. Rather, this person who clings to such a faith has eternal life within oneself, and because this life is eternal, this person also keeps it.

Yet, my good friends, suppose that this were everything, namely, the soul's gradual healing from corruption by faith in the Lord, a person's gradual growth in one's similarity to him, and the ever more regulating possession of internal human salvation. To be sure, that would be a great good, but it would not be the supreme good for which the Lord appeared. This is so, my good friends, for something specific and greater lies in the expression "to save," namely, in an original way God alone is blessed, or saved, Supreme Being, Who lacks nothing, Who is self-sufficient, not needing anything. We are not like this in and of ourselves, not in a state of healing, not in a state of sin's disappearance, not in a state in which we still look up at the Redeemer and receive the power of blessedness, or salvation, from him. Rather, we would be all of that only if no separation between us and our Lord were to exist anymore. We are that now only in unity with him, a unity that is like his unity with the Father, a unity in which also he alone was saved.[13] This is so, for we must also ascribe to the only Son of God this specific and original blessing, or salvation, and it is precisely his glory that shines toward us, for only from him who is blessed, or saved, within oneself are we able to take and to draw continually grace after grace from his fullness.[14]

13. John 17: 22, 23.
14. John 1:16.

Yet, it is not the just born human child who gradually advanced in age and wisdom and grace[15] that is the one who is blessed, or saved, within himself. Rather, he is that by virtue of the fullness of divinity that dwelled within him.[16] He is that by virtue of being one with his Father,[17] a condition which he gave us as a sign that he was sent by his Father and as a sign that the power that blesses was in himself. So too we are blessed, or saved, only in the immediate oneness with him that is effected by the faith dwelling in our hearts, only by our feeling within us his immediate presence and his immediate power, only by our being aware of the Spirit, which he breathed into his own and from which we know that he is given to each person by God through faith. In this way, we are blessed, or saved, not in ourselves but in him. That condition to which faith in him is to lead us, however, is also nothing less than precisely this blessedness, or salvation.

Furthermore, my good friends, being such a sign of God's love as can be compared with nothing else—love destined to bring eternal life and blessing, or salvation, by faith—the Redeemer then presents himself as the general good of humankind. This is so, for the last words of our text—"the Son of God was sent not to condemn the world but to save the world"—are directed against a prejudice very widely disseminated amid the people among whom the Redeemer was born and lived, namely, the prejudice that when God's especially consecrated one would appear, at first he would also be only a particular good of the chosen people, and that by leading them back to their original glory, he would pass strict judgment against all peoples who ever had hostilely opposed God's own people. From the soul of Nicodemus and from all the souls to whom he might report regarding the teacher sent by God the Redeemer wants to banish this erroneous idea by saying that the Son of God was sent not to condemn the world but to save it. Accordingly, he thereby wants to be considered one by whose agency no evil of any kind should befall anyone, who also did not come to bring any evil consequence of sin that is perpetrated upon certain people while he blesses, heals, and saves others. Rather, by saying whoever believes in him has eternal life and will not be condemned because this person has eternal life, but the person who does not have faith or believe, is already condemned, for that person

15. Luke 2:52.
16. Col 2:9.
17. John 10:30.

does not have faith or believe, in the name of the only Son of God,[18] he is saying that nothing will befall those who do not have faith in him other than what would already have befallen them if he had not appeared. The condemnation is nothing other than this: a lack of faith in the Son of the living God.

So, my good friends, he juxtaposes salvation and lack of salvation, or blessedness and lack thereof, in such a way that each contrasting emotive state thereby becomes clear to us. That is, on the one hand, there is blessedness, or salvation, possession of the light and of the entire splendor that attends it in eternal life, and, on the other hand, there is the lack of blessedness, or salvation, having nonfaith, the entire nature of the darkness that lies in the lack of faith. We know, as the greatest distinction that there can be, this one: To be blessed, or saved, and to be condemned; and as this greatest distinction the Lord here represents those who have faith in him and those who do not have faith in him. Yes, my good friends, how could it be otherwise? On the one hand, to have faith in the Redeemer means to have faith in the immediate unity of God with human nature in his person, whereby in turn a connection of all those persons who have faith in him and who adhere to him came to be possible on God's part. On the other hand, however, not to have faith in him, thus to believe that there is no such connection of God with humankind, that eternal Being continues to stay far away from humankind and continually distances itself from it—in his life and what he says the Redeemer juxtaposes each of these conditions for us, as the greatest possible contrast. The person who has faith in the one Redeemer thereby has passed through from death to eternal life.[19] This is so, for what greater and more splendid consciousness can there be than that of such a unity with God as gives us a blessedness, or salvation, that is to be compared with nothing else? Yet, what a state of forlornness it is to be far removed from this faith! Further, how must we not say of what help it would be to an individual if one gained heaven and earth[20] but could not believe in this love of God toward human beings, this love of God who sent God's only Son to unite human beings with Godself!

My good friends, what we have considered with one another now, so as to animate the proper Christmas joy within us, is the proper witness

18. John 5:24.
19. John 5:24.
20. Matt 16:26.

that the Son of God bore of himself. He himself says, "If I testify concerning myself, and if people do not accept it, then this response can be
justifiable, because even if anyone should speak truth when one speaks
of oneself, this can always be of little consequence."[21] In contrast, if the
Son of God gives evidence of himself, it is the immortal image of the
Father that speaks to us in the works of nature and that lives in the Word
of Scripture and in immediate, living revelation by the Son of God. In
concert, his thoroughgoing revelation testifies for him and provides con-
firmation of any self-testimony to or by him. Accordingly, just as to the
woman who first announced to certain Samaritans that she had found
the Messiah, the Samaritans said that they could no longer believe for her
word's sake but because they themselves had heard and had known that
this Christ was present as the Savior of the world, so too everyone who
has faith in the Lord may and must say that they believe no longer for the
sake of some testimony, also not even for the sake of the testimony that
he himself delivered, but because they themselves have had experience
of him!

Yes, my good friends, we must experience the glory of the only Son.
We must experience this love of God toward humankind, that God sent
God's Son into the world to bless, or save, the world. We must experience
this blessing, or salvation, and eternal life itself, the feeling that we will
not perish and that nothing can separate us from the love of God[22] if we
remain in the love of the one whom God has sent! Amen.

21. John 5:31 (NRSV).
22. Rom 8:35, 39.

6

The Dayspring [Dawn] from on High

The First Day of Christmas
Saturday, December 25, 1824[1]

Glory to God in the Highest and on Earth
Peace to People of Good Will.

By the tender mercy of our God,
    the dawn from on high will break upon us,
To give light to those who sit in darkness
        and the shadow of death,
    to guide our feet into the way of peace.

—LUKE 1:78, 79 (NRSV)

My devout friends, this is a voice concerning our Redeemer, a voice that rings over to us from Old Testament times, long before Jesus' birth. It is a voice spoken by the father of him who was the precursor [John the Baptist] of our Lord [Jesus] but designating Jesus as the Lord ahead of whom that other infant was to walk so as to prepare the way for him. Further,

---

1. In the "early sermons" of that period, Schleiermacher was continuously treating the Gospel of John, near Christmas Day, here John 6, within a long series on that Gospel, and he had chosen the present text for Christmas Day. The final copy contains numerous orthographic changes and small spelling mistakes that had been corrected, otherwise revised only slightly, by him. It was first published by Johannes Bauer, *Schleiermacher als patriotischer Prediger* (1908), 74–81, notetaker not identified.

it is a voice well suited to lead our festive reflection today. This is so, for we have already heard so many themes that are admired alongside each other, themes based on which we would explore a good many specific reasons for the festive joy that we feel today and that we would now consider more closely. The Lord, whose birth we celebrate, visited us as "the dawn [dayspring] from on high" because of God's mercy. This same Lord has shone on all those who sit "in darkness and in the shadow of death." Finally, the Lord "guides our feet into the way of peace."

I

Thus, first, "the dayspring from on high" visited us because of the mercy of God. The dayspring from on high, my devout friends, this is a beautiful expression for explaining the relationship of our Lord to all who have faith in him. First, it designates his heavenly origin, but then, at the same time, it also designates that he has been the object of longing and of hope. That is to say, my dear friends, at all times human beings have looked toward heaven in feeling their imperfect and helpless condition, and they have set their gaze toward what comes from "on high" and toward morning.

To be sure, in part, humans have also gazed toward evening. That is, they have directed their glances to what is past in a more or less definitive feeling that their current state at a given time was not the original one; yet, because it is to be viewed as a matter of corruption, a better one must have preceded it. Thus, they have directed the eyes of their spirit to that better condition as to a setting sun, and, as best they could, they have sought to make images of the past that they had no longer held. However, my good friends, it was not that from where blessedness, or salvation, could come. Rather, by doing this image making, human beings had to be put ever more into the darkness and into the shadow of death if they were to seek life and light in what is past, in some past from which nothing helpful was to be found. Thus, it was the hope—it was the joyful, albeit darkened trust in God—that there would still be a help and rest that would have been driving human beings to gaze toward morning for their future.

Humans are not to look to the earth, however; for corruption, and the feeling of corruption, was so fully universal that they all indeed became aware that what was earthly could not help them. This was and is so, for even if along with their thoughts they could comprehend what is best, most noble, and most excellent, nevertheless what they actually saw was always simply the same decrepitude, always simply the same inability, always simply the same defilement—all of which are brought about by sin. It was only the "dayspring from on high" to which they could direct their hopes and wishes. What was to prepare true help for them would have to have come down from above, but then would subsequently also have to have continued to shine and radiate on earth. Accordingly, in his presentiment of the one for whom his son was to prepare the way, Zechariah then said that because of God's mercy the dayspring from on high has visited us, for the future seemed so near and so very present to him.

For God's dayspring to visit and/or to make a visit, my good friends, we know this from Scripture to be a designation of a closer relationship into which God places Godself with humankind and under certain conditions. The Scriptures of the Old Testament are full of divine visitations that bear the image of divine wrath. Yet, no voice that resounds to us from on high is more joyful than when, as was once said, "The Lord [God] has looked favorably on the Lord's people,"[2] for, if divine wrath and divine punishment are not explicitly added, then, according to the sense given to the phrase within that period, one would not be able to take this allusion otherwise than to trace the visitation of the Lord back to divine grace and mercy.

Yet, my good friends, God had never before visited humankind in such a way as God did when God sent us the "dayspring from on high." That is to say, on account of that visit everything that the human soul would ever appropriate in hope would then become its own and would be present for all times. Because of the dayspring, or dawn, from on high, we are now visited by God in such a way that we are to be at one with God, as God was at one with him whom God sent, so that with and because of the only begotten Son of God we are all to be children of God—children such that from them God's grace and faithfulness, God's very truth and love, could never be removed again.

2. In the RSV and other earlier editions, "has visited"; whereas in the NRSV (1989) "has looked favorably on," which is more in keeping with Schleiermacher's meaning. See the NRSV footnote. John the Baptist's father, Zechariah, speaks this lengthy prayer and prophetic utterance (Luke 1:68–79) regarding "the "Lord God of Israel"—the Benedictus, as it has been termed traditionally. The Hebrew verb for "visit," or "look favorably on," is frequently used throughout the Old Testament, as is its Greek equivalent in several key places within the New Testament. Here the action that Zechariah cannily prophesies for the baby Jesus places "and redeems them" after "the Lord's people" (Israel).

Moreover, suppose that we might think that after the Lord had, in turn, left this earthly scene, there would be yet another visitation that God would present and offer in explanation.[3] Suppose too that this would not be another visible appearance on earth as well but would be an invisible power that the Lord would be planting into human souls, namely the visitation by the Lord's Spirit when the Lord would pour it out over all sorts of flesh, a word, as it were, spoken from the beginning of his final days. Nevertheless, my good friends, this visitation would be nothing but a continuation of the same visitation. That is, it would be the union of God with the human soul for the sake of which the Lord had come, and God could not have visited us in this way if the only begotten Son of the Father had not previously appeared as the real and sole dayspring from on high. This is so, for what the Spirit of God is and effects within and among God's persons of faith is something that refers to all God's own. Regarding his own the Lord himself said that he would take them up in order to give them God's Spirit and to illumine them.[4]

Moreover, if we think of this and give God the honor in that the dayspring from on high has visited us, how could we do otherwise than also ascribe it, as Zechariah also did, to the tender mercy of God? To be sure, my good friends, in God properties, virtues, and perfections are not something particular, separated, and divided. Rather, they are all one and the same.[5] In the human domain nothing that is good and excellent is to be distinguished from each other more than are justice and mercy, but in God, my good friends, even these two attributes are one and the same. We can, indeed we could, just as well say this: Because of the justice of our God, it has happened that the dayspring from on high has visited us. This would be so, my good friends, for when from the beginning of things, as the Lord God saw everything that the Lord had made, the Lord said that everything was "good," how indeed could we say that at that time the Lord did not see the darkness and the shadow of death, into which human beings would sink? Further, if, in spite of this, the Lord said, everything is good, thereby how was the Lord not also to have been aware of the redemption that the Lord wanted to prepare for humankind precisely through the visitation of the dayspring from on high? Moreover,

---

3. John 16:14 (NRSV): "He will glorify me, because he will take from what is mine and declare it to you."

4. John 15:26 and in John 16.

5. *Christian Faith* (2016), §64ff. Here the "image" cannot be strictly that of "mercy" (ibid., §85), because that would involve modeling God's image after that of humankind.

as the two things, sin and redemption, were enclosed in the Lord God's eternal decree, the Lord could, indeed, do nothing other than also provide redemption after sin had established itself. Furthermore, it is nothing other than that the Lord manifested the Lord's truth and justice when the Lord visited sinful humankind, which had, indeed, been created in conformity with the Lord's image, an image that was to be like that of the Lord, through the dayspring from on high and bringing humankind to a happiness that the Lord would not be in position to previously offer.[6]

We, however, my good friends, who know ourselves and are conscious of ourselves as spontaneous, self-active beings, at the same time also do, indeed, know and feel that by our own power we are not capable of reaching the goal that was present in every era within the minds of human beings looking to the morning and toward what is on high. Nonetheless, we cannot get rid of the consciousness that this is our goal and that we are to reach it. We can do nothing other than to be suffused by consciousness that even if we should come to be incapable of reaching our goal, we would have nothing more to require of God after God had endowed the human soul as an image that is like God's. Further, because we know that we have no claim on God, but that we would also have been capable of reaching our goal by the original use of powers placed within us, we cannot do anything other than to ascribe this result to God's mercy, that the dayspring from on high broke upon us. Accordingly, it is thus humanly spoken and in a human manner when even here, should the word of those men from the Old Testament times be included in Scripture, the process is especially attributed to God's mercy.[7]

However, for us, my good friends, this process is explained in an even more elevated fashion if we recall how this is one of the treasures of wisdom that we likewise owe only to the dayspring from on high, namely,

6. See *Christian Faith* (2016), §106.2. This passage indicates that ascribing mercy to God is more suited to the domain of homiletic and poetic discourse than to that of dogmatic language, as the anthropopathic reference, which can hardly be separated from it, shows well enough. God's mercy is to be understood as nothing other than God's love and justice, simply seen from a different perspective. Cf. the October 24, 1830, sermon "That We Have Nothing to Learn from God's Wrath," the ninth of ten critically minded sermons preached on the handing over to the king of the Augsburg Confession (1530), with a preface largely regarding previous criticisms of his earlier publications on uses of creeds and confessions in the church. See Tice, *Schleiermacher's Sermons* (1997), 98–101, including the numerous editions of the whole set of sermons; and see Schleiermacher, *Reformed but Ever Reforming* (ET: Nicol [1997]).

7. Schleiermacher uses the term *mercy* in this sermon during worship, if not in his dogmatics, as a gesture toward custom. See *Christian Faith* (2016), 85.

that we know God is love. In mercy, by virtue of which the dayspring from on high broke upon us, divine love is, to be sure, reflected in our disposition and in our feeling as the very nature of the omnipotent and eternal God, and our being invested in this disposition and feeling is the reason that the dayspring from on high has visited us. It is the work of God's love that the Word became flesh and dwelt among us. It is the work of God's love that we, we who once could not bear to see the Lord's countenance, now see the glory of God in the glory of the only begotten Son of the Father. Accordingly, the dayspring from on high visited us so that our eyes would now be opened and purified, so, with the result that we could see the Father in the Son and in this way that we could return with him into the living community of the divine Spirit.

II

Further, what we still need to do, my good friends, is first to explain to ourselves in detail the following words of our text, that the dayspring from on high broke upon us to shine light on those who are sitting there in darkness and the shadow of death. Simply one thing, my good friends, especially has to strike us here, namely: we cannot know with how clear or dark a consciousness John the Baptist's father was thinking when he spoke the words he did. This is so, for he must have been thinking, above all, of his own people, viewed as the people from ancient times who were chosen by God, as the people to whom divine promises were given. Through the possession of these promises—even if their fulfillment at times seemed to move near, and at times seemed, in turn, to withdraw farther back—these people were already distinguished from all other groups of human beings and were raised above them. He was thinking especially of his people viewed as those who, robbed of their former glory, having declined by a condition of blood and force, were now to be seen more as a people who were sitting in darkness and in the shadow of death. However, for us, my good friends, this distinction has disappeared. There is such bliss and fullness in the blessedness, or salvation, that has come about for humankind through the visit of the dayspring from on high that the distinction between those who enjoy this blessing and those who are still far from it is simply that of the greatest people—no, we must say instead the only people—that now exist among human beings and in light of which all other distinctions disappear and are not to be taken into account.[8]

It is true, however, that all of us, the entirety of humankind, have sat in darkness and in the shadow of death.[9] What that description intends to say, my good friends, that we do indeed feel. The light is what is clear, the light is what is pleasant and blissful, in which light we also perceive everything, and only in this light are we able to live and to have an effect as long as day will have existed. In contrast, darkness and the shadow of death comprise all that is lacking in pleasure.[10] It is that wherein we are robbed of the use of our powers, if any such state occurs within us. It is the opposite of all life, of all joy and of all efficacy. Moreover, the human condition is indeed rightly described in this way and in no other, if we are to think of human beings as independent of the actual appearance of the dayspring from on high. This would be the case, no matter whether humans were existing before or at the appearance of the dayspring or afterward. Consider, further, how the Lord himself stated this observation and confirmed it when he said: "I am a light come into the world so that anyone who has faith in me does not remain in darkness."[11] At that point, did he not say very clearly that all who do not have faith in him dwell in darkness? However, those who have faith in him, my good friends, are the people who know him and rejoice in him as the dayspring from on high! They are the people who hear the words that he received from the Father and spoke, the words that are spirit and life. They are the people into whose hearts the will of God, which he revealed to us, penetrated, but who also know that only if they come to the one who calls those who suffer and are burdened to himself and who know that only if they are still shoots on the vine, shoots in which divine forces bring fullness, are they able to do the Father's will and to hold fast in their very souls the voices of life that he spoke!

8. Schleiermacher is claiming that while once the Jewish people could think of themselves as the "greatest" because of God's covenant with them, now Christians should say of themselves, because they now constitute "the new creation" in Christ, that they are the "only" people who are specially blessed, even if all human beings—Jews, Gentiles and all—are somehow eventually to be "saved" in Schleiermacher's prophetic doctrine of universal salvation.

9. See *Christian Faith* (2016), §§59–85.

10. See *Christian Faith* (2016), Analytical Index under "pleasure" (*Lust* and its contrast *Unlust*).

11. John 8:12; NRSV: "will never walk in darkness." See also *Christian Faith* (2016) §§35–36, §46 and §107.4.

Now, these voices are light and life. The light, as the apostle John says at the beginning of his Gospel, has always shone into the darkness; shining into the darkness was that which sought to penetrate the darkness from within itself, and which turned the eyes of human beings toward the dawn and toward what is on high. However, the time did come when the light could not penetrate the darkness, and the darkness could not receive it. Precisely on this account, there is no description for such a human condition other than darkness and the shadow of death. The Lord came and appeared, nevertheless, as a light to all those who would be sitting in darkness and the shadow of death. How he does continually illuminate, how he does, in turn, make earthly life clear and friendly, how he does deliver us from the darkness in which we find our very eyes darkened and our power paralysed![12]

Let us never forget, however, that without him we would still be sitting in darkness and the shadow of death, that the powers that God placed into human souls could not be released and set free save through the help brought by the dayspring from on high. Let us not forget this gift, so that we can entirely give to God and to the tender mercy of God the honor that is due God for having sent us the one who continuously visits us as the dayspring from on high. Yet now, my good friends, the light has appeared! Now everywhere the darkness and the shadow of death are also to vanish, and the life of human beings is to become ever friendlier, brighter, and more blessed, and the dayspring from on high is to shine ever farther and its light is to spread over the entire earth and over all areas inhabited by humankind.

III

Ultimately, he appeared to us in order to guide our feet into the way of peace. This gift of peace, my good friends, the Lord himself quite especially commends to us, presenting it as the entire content of what he can give to humankind. He said: "I do not give to you as the world gives. I give to you my peace, I leave my peace to you."[13] In this way he himself verifies these words, that he came in order to guide our feet into the way of peace.

12. See the 1823 Christmas sermon on John 3:16–28, Thursday, December 25 and especially that on the following Sunday, December 28, on John 3: 19–21, in SW II.8 (1837), 197–206. These sermons, unlike that from 1820, are not yet available in English translation.

13. John 14:27 (NRSV). *Christian Faith* (2016), Analytical Index under "peace."

However, my good friends, one may ask: How is this peace present-ed to us in this passage? It is presented as a path that we have available to walk upon, that is, as a good that can be achieved only in activity and in the proper use of our powers, as a good that is not just possessed, as if it were something that simply comes from outside but for which one must constantly strive and to which one must constantly aspire, which one has to gain by striving and aspiring. This is so, for it is said: "He guides our feet into the way of peace." If the Lord himself then says, "Blessed are the peacemakers who gladly place their feet on the way of peace and would follow no other than this pathway, then they are blessed, for they will be called the children of God."[14] We know, my good friends, that to be a child of God is indeed to be seen, on the one hand, not as an activity that we can acquire and obtain for ourselves by simply walking on this or that path. No, only through him, the only begotten Son, are we called and are we the children of God! This is the strength that he gave to all those who have faith in him, and being a child of God consists in our having faith in him. Moreover, this childlike relationship to God is a gift of the one who in himself having faith in and through God called us to life and made faith subject to a word spoken in the Gospels.

Yet, it is the Spirit that comes from God that calls out "dear Father" within us. It is by virtue of God's Spirit in which we have a childlike relationship with God and which we have received as the Spirit of this childlike relationship. This divine Spirit, however, is indeed the divine power that suffuses and animates everyone who has faith in Christ our Lord, and all efficacy of the divine Spirit in our souls is indeed nothing other than our way of living and the leading of our feet into the way of peace. Thus, we walk in the world through the strength of God's Spirit as children of God. Thereby the peace of the Lord is also sure to be within us. This is so, for we are children of God in him and through him, and we are so inasmuch as we are one in the Spirit, for peace is where unity of the Spirit lies, and therein we are the children of God. This has oc-curred because God dwelled within our Lord and reconciled the world with Godself through him, and it has also occurred because as we are at one with him, we are also at one with the Father, and the Father comes to dwell in our hearts. Alternately spoken, the peace of God exists where God's dwelling with the Son is in our hearts, where being at one with the Father exists through the Son. However, it is this very peace of God that is higher than any reason, that also cannot be comprehended and cannot

14. Matt 5:9 (NRSV).

be engendered by anyone. Instead, the gift is of the Spirit that the Son has sent, of the Spirit of truth and of the Spirit of our childlike relationship with God.[15]

Now then, my good friends, let us enjoy the heavenly gifts that have come to us through the dayspring from on high's having visited us! May honor be to him who visits humankind in this way! However, if it is he who guides our feet into the way of peace, then, my friends, may peace on earth also thrive among all those who follow on his pathway and to whom he has become truth and life! May this be so precisely because he showed them the way and also gives them the strength to walk on it! Also, may the divine peace that the Lord brought hold sway everywhere, so that in place of darkness and the shadow of death an eternal and joyful pleasure may spread among all who know the dayspring from on high, among all who have received the light that shone into the darkness and who have come to be its own light, among all who, as such, have received the strength to be the children of God in their holding faith in him! Amen.

※

Editor's Postscript

Are these really sermons? Yes, they really are, and in those days they took about forty-five minutes to deliver. Once revised and readied for readers, moreover, they have always seemed to me more like treatises as Schleiermacher thought them out—and to recall that in the pulpit they had all started out as mere outlines, written with whatever he used for a pen in tiny script laying out but a few major points! As I have come to envisage him in the pulpit—keen-eyed and calm but emotively engaged, in his typically complex, but smoothly unloaded discourse—he was always sharing with his "listening" and "devout" friends, as he called them (and us!) concerning their inner faith (such as it might be), their life, and their consequent belief. Such careful listening and devout friends might have seen him strong-shouldered and (in later years) slight, his large face cropped with thick-flowing blond or white hair; they would

15. This final section has been both an extension of what Schleiermacher wrote in passages regarding "new life" and "peace" in *Christian Faith*. See *Christian Faith* (2016), Analytical Index on those topics and a bridge to his *Christian Ethics*, on which he was working especially hard during the mid-1820s.

have seen him dressed in coal-black garments with Geneva tabs and climbing (deftly as an athlete) the narrow stairs to his high pulpit. There Schleiermacher preached, literally standing against one wall of a towering, totally round sanctuary noticeable from a mile away, set atop a busy city street that sloped gently up to the church for several blocks. Directly he faced mostly a third gallery of free-seated folk, mostly visitors and former peasant families. (These had been peasants since 1813, when the king had emancipated them to keep them on his side during the war with Napoleon, whose army had been defeated in a battle just outside Hallesches Tor tower at a far corner of their parish; the parish itself was walled and gated at the end of one long side.) From the pulpit he would also have to encompass in his gaze all the rest of his audience somewhat below, sitting for the most part in rental seats. By custom, the large outer doors were closed to drown out the racket of wagons and carriages against cobblestones.

So, the remaining sermons in this volume were all prepared and offered after his masterpiece *Christian Faith* was published in its second, final edition (1830–1831). Viewed as whole, the full set of eleven Christmas sermons gathered here includes a number of insights and nonpummeling challenges. I trust that you are willing to take them in as well, for you are likely to be inspired to futher reflection by them all.

7

Joy in Christ's Appearance, Enhanced by the Observation that He Has Come to Bring a Sword

Second Day of Christmas
Sunday, December 26, 1824[1]

Glory to God in the highest, and on earth peace
to human beings with whom God is well-pleased. Amen.

> Do not think that I have come to bring peace to the earth;
> I have come not to bring peace, but a sword.
> —MATTHEW 10:34 (NRSV)

My devout friends. How astoundingly dissonant these words of the Lord resound in the angelic greeting that we would have heard immediately before, so that they threaten to blot out for us the entire joy and blessedness of this festival. This is so, for its reference to a "sword" is especially directed to the honor of God, and we may ask: If that greeting rages afresh, does that reference to a sword entail a particular approval for that reference by and among human beings? Now, if peace coming to the earth is said to mean from heaven downward, how can the Lord himself say: "Do

---

1. This 1824 sermon first appeared in *Christliche Festpredigten* (1826), 111–37, then in SW II.2 (1834, 1843), 69–84; see an earlier ET: Wilson, *Selected Sermons of Schleiermacher* (1890), 295–313.

not think that I have come to bring peace but a sword"? Moreover, we must also ask: If what he said then is true, should we not seek, most of all, to conceal this dismal truth and to remove it from our souls precisely on the days of joy concerning his coming? Surely not, for it has already long been the custom in a large part of the Christian church to commemorate on the second day of Christmas the memory of that first martyr, who died in the name of the Lord.[2] This was indeed at a time when the word of the Lord was beginning to be fulfilled. So, we might well wonder further: Why, then, my devout friends, have these two things, festive joy and use of the sword, been moved so close together? Does not precisely this conjuncture seem to be expressed therein, namely, that the birth of martyrdom is, so to speak, the next and most immediate glorification of Christ's very birth? Indeed, we should know (and precisely in these days especially remember), just as we do otherwise recall what it cost him, so now in particular we should remember what his appearance has brought to us—I mean, what it has brought to the entirety of humankind, notably insofar as it is made up of persons of faith. It has brought crowns of victory from the beginning of Christ's moving onward, namely, in that we are redeemed by him in such a costly manner. We should include in this account all suffering that people have endured for his name's sake, all misery that has befallen his own persons of faith and his first disciples, every instance of discord that has been spread over the earth in quarrels over his name. Should we not bear all this in mind when we celebrate his coming? By these tokens we should know him: His rising among us from on high, his being the one who has visited us, and his operating as the prince of peace, who also directs our feet onto the path of peace.[3]

Well! In this way, then, we do not want to be afraid to attach the serious and important word of the Lord to our Christmas joy; rather, by this reflection that the Lord has come to bring a sword we want to try to elevate and purify our joy in his coming. For this festive hour it is this to which I implore your Christian devotion and attentiveness. What matters in adopting this focus, however, is this: First, that the Lord has come to bring a sword to earth most surely ensures that he also truly became our brother inasmuch as his entire life and activity was subject

2. In Acts Stephen was reported to have been among seven early disciples selected to serve tables. He was a notably devout man, later stoned to death, then referred to as a martyr. Tradition has it that he was the first Christian martyr. As Saint Stephen he also represents an original diaconal ministry in the Christian church.

3. See especially Luke 1:79 and 2:14ff; also John 14:27.

to all conditions of truly human activity; second, we find in the fact that he came to bring a sword on earth the best assurance for the fullness of divinity having indeed indwelled him; and, finally, that he came to bring a sword gives us the most comforting assurance concerning the unshakable steadfastness of the union between him and us. Let us now consider all of these things more closely, each point in succession.

I

First, my good friends, I would say that the greatest surety for the Lord's life and activity lies in his having been truly human from the beginning, which does ensure for us precisely that he could not refrain from bringing a sword to earth. This would be the case, for how do human beings conduct themselves with respect to everything that is pressed upon them in a human manner? Imparted to them viewed as the lasting sign of their fragility is the error to which they—however well-meaning they might be, and however much they might aspire to what is good—unfortunately did indeed always remain so subject to errant behavior that error could readily sneak up on them unexpectedly. Hence, my good friends, a given human being can be blinded toward and about everything that is presented to oneself by others. For example, what is most beneficent can appear dangerous to someone; what is most salutary can appear ruinous to another; what is itself divine can appear and lacking in pleasure perverse to someone else. Now, if the Lord's activity was itself supposed to be truly human, without any secret force turning round the usual manner of all human mental interaction, then to some people even the Redeemer would have had to be subject to these conditions of all human activity. Thus, when evil spirits gave way before him, they thought that this could happen in no other manner. That is, some among the witnesses of his acts had to be so blinded concerning him and his existence that they thought he would drive out evil spirits only by means of one who is supreme over the evil spirits themselves. When this rumor about him began to spread and people were quietly and, as it were, surreptitiously whispering into each other's ears the notion that this Jesus of Nazareth might not be the one who was to come, namely the helper, the Savior, the Messiah, to them this activity could happen in no other way. Even among his own people some, though familiar with the divine promises that had been imparted to these people over a long series of generations, had to be so blinded concerning him that even the signs and indications of their Scripture would simply confirm them in their blindness. Thus, it came about that some said: "If Christ will come, we will not know whence he comes; about this one, however, we know whence he comes and know his father and his mother and his brothers and his sisters." Others would hold to a different prejudice and would say: "Is he not from Nazareth, and have you ever heard that a prophet has arisen or is to rise from Galilee?" This, my good friends, this had to be the destiny of the Redeemer as soon as his activity was meant to be genuinely and purely human. Moreover, based precisely on this sightedness of individuals who wanted to find salvation on a different path than one wherever it is alone to be assuredly and lastingly found, it therefore came to pass that he brought a sword to the earth, that for his sake parents would arm themselves, as it were, against their children and children against their parents, that siblings and friends would arm themselves against one another.

How would human beings conduct themselves toward everything that affects them in a human way? As soon as the subject of discussion is the innermost nature of being human, we know that we are like one another. However, the same thing that befalls several, that thing, at the same time, stimulates many, indeed affects them in a very different way, depending either on whether one is placed in a certain position and another is placed differently in general terms; or on whether, in particular respects, one is disposed to live in one way and another in some other way. Thus, the situation could not be otherwise than that both the Lord himself, as long as he lived on earth, as well as the word of some sermon that he might have founded in his church, once he was no longer physically present, would always have affected people differently. So, when it was preached to some that Jesus, whom they had delivered up and killed, had been made a Lord and Christ by God and that blessedness, or salvation, and forgiveness of sins is to be found only in his name, these words touched people's hearts and they asked: What, then, should we do, so that we may find blessedness, or salvation? Yet, how many others would have remained indifferent to these claims, would have shook their heads, and would have left the premises just as they had come to them?

Now, if people's arousal is so different, my good friends, ah, is this difference not also something completely human, then, such that someone who has remained indifferent would consider another more moved in mind and heart and would then gladly take everything received along into this same indifferent state for no gain other than to become an enemy of someone else's peace of mind? Precisely because people react differently to the same teaching, circumstances like this have cropped up from the very outset on. Ever since the word of reconciliation began to be proclaimed, there have been people who did not want to be disturbed in their peace of mind by this word, in relation to which they, to be sure, simply sat in darkness and in the shadow of death, but yet they had to find themselves reliably encountered and well-advised until, at last, some movement of the divine toward them would have penetrated even into their perhaps thus far impenitent hearts!

Hence, the situation could not be otherwise than that whoever would cause a movement toward people such as the Redeemer would also have to bring a sword to the earth. This would be so, my good friends, for if someday people were to split one from another but they would then still restrain themselves in that split and remain within certain limits, with the results that the situation would not come down to such violent scenes, feuds, and ravages as are typically designated by the expression "sword," then what would the reason for this eventuality be but that they would not consider the subject to be important enough? Yet, even if the life and activity of the Lord would actually be so very much subject to all these limitations of human activity, at least this feature did also necessarily belong among them. That is to say, the movement to which he gave rise on earth had to appear to everyone, the longer time went on the more so, more momentous than any other movement to which they had ever been led! Otherwise, the reign of God too could not have emerged from it. Therefore, also the split of differently disposed persons that his coming aroused and subsequently the message regarding him brought forth would together have been violent enough everywhere to deserve the expression that he came to bring a sword to the earth, and without exception we would see this sword raging—sometimes more, sometimes less cruelly and destructively—wherever the word of peace would be proclaimed. Thus, my good friends, if the process had been different, how, then, would the whole matter have stood? Then the word of the apostle too could not have been true. Once he said: When the fullness of time had come, God sent his Son, born of a woman and under the law,[4] this might have meant that because not enough receptivity had yet been awakened for the subject of his sending, so that he could markedly stir people and intensely move them either to approval or to disapproval. In contrast,

4. Gal 4:4.

when within human history the time had come so far that wherever the Redeemer appeared he also brought the burning sword: Then the time was truly fulfilled; then he could appear as the Redeemer!

It is good for us, moreover, that he did appear at this time, my good friends! Or perhaps should his coming have been delayed until it would no longer have been necessary for him to bring a sword along with the promise of peace, until every blessing of his coming could have taken place mildly and amiably without people's destructive, retrograde movements? No, suppose that by themselves and without him people had been able to come so far that they would have devolved directly into a divine life and into a heavenly light without division and without disunity, just as had been shown to them. Then, truly, they could also have found all that for themselves, and the Redeemer's coming would no longer have been necessary.

Now, if precisely this course of events did not and could not occur, then we would still be sitting in darkness and in the shadow of death, and thousands of generations could still pass away. Right along during that period, blessedness, or salvation, would still not have arisen. Thus, a proper blessedness, or salvation, either could not be brought forth at all or could be brought forth in such a way that the Savior of the world would first have had to bring a sword before the peace that he actually left for his own could spread his blessings over them. Thus, in this respect the stern and cutting word of the Redeemer, that he came to bring a sword, exactly concurs with the milder sounding word of the apostle that was already cited, that he was to be born of a woman and under the law. That is to say, in the law of his people everything that resembled magic,[5] every use of any mysterious power was most strictly prohibited. So, even the Redeemer would have been limited to the naturally effective mode of his mind, precisely because he was born under the law. If it were to have been otherwise, my good friends, if he had drawn minds and hearts to himself in a way other than by genuinely human influence, then he could also not have been our brother, because the divine force within him would have used instruments and means other than his human nature but would have pushed it to the side, viewed as useless. Furthermore, we also could not boast, in the sense that we so gladly do, that in Christ the rising from

5. By now, Schleiermacher had fully concealed the contrary-to-natural concept "magic" (and "magical") in relation to healthier concepts used in his theological and philosophical discourses. See *Christian Faith* (2016) Analytical Index, for a definition and discussions of "magic."

on high also came to us, or visited us, for this fine and pleasing word indeed means nothing less than that the rising from on high, as it would eventually have appeared in our homeland, also stepped completely into the order of our life and in no way other than one of us having an effect in this earthly world, where everything that we have explained thus far would be simply natural, and all that can first cease to be simply natural and in the natural order would be so when his work is accomplished at days' end.

Thus, my good friends, in that we rejoice in him and in his coming, we would also want to rejoice that he came born of a woman and under the law, also that his redeeming activity, or his beneficial effect, could not be other than this: To bring a sword to the earth!

II

Second, and in contrast, this account is likewise a sure guarantee that the fullness of divinity dwelt within him and that the one who visited us truly was the rising from on high. This is so, my good friends, for as we know, based on the words of our text and from so many other expressions of the Lord, this indwelling of divinity was not concealed from him. Indeed, he knew it and foresaw it most exactly. He, who had entered so deeply into the very nature of human beings and of the human heart, as even into the particular circumstances of his era, knew that he brought a sword to the earth. Furthermore, he did indeed come, and he came in the way he did, because it was not possible to do his redemptive work otherwise. That is, otherwise he could indeed not fail to redeem humankind and to free those who were sitting there in darkness and in the shadow of death!

My good friends, just recall the story that the Lord told to his disciples about how he was tempted in the desert. Consider how, precisely in that he rejected so purely and simply each seductive suggestion, we all find in this story the clearest proof of the purity of the divine force that lived within him. Moreover, let us then envisage which of those temptations actually were as they were narrated to us in that passage. In contrast, imagine that the tempter had come to him, and instead of showing him, at the peak of the mountain, the kingdoms of the world and their glory,[6] the tempter would have shown him the streams of blood that would flow on earth for his name's sake. Thereby the tempter would

6. Matt 4:8; Luke 4:5–6.

have shown him not, as it were, his own cross but how this cross would multiply ad infinitum for the entire group of his faithful confessors and disciples. The tempter would have shown him how a burning sword would snatch away thousands upon thousands, and the band of bondage in which his witnesses would have to sigh, and all the shame and scorn of the world, all the pains and privations of love. Suppose that the tempter had shown him the entire rage of persecution that would come down on his witnesses, more severely than the servitude from which Moses freed the people of the old covenant with his strong hand. Then, finally, would the tempter have shown him the heartrending destruction of the most very sacred of human relations for his name's sake? Moreover, if the tempter had already shown him all this in one dark image embracing centuries and millennia, after that would he have briskly taunted him as to whether he was also reflecting on all this? And yet would the tempter also have been firmly determined to bring this immense mass of misery and wretchedness upon humankind in addition to all the suffering they would already have had to endure anyway, deservedly or undeservedly? Suppose that the tempter had then asked Jesus Christ whether he was sure that the blessedness, or salvation, that Christ had imagined finding among his witnesses would offset all this anguish; whether indeed in such a way that his witnesses, in turn, would spoil it by an inclination toward the delusion and error ingrained in them from ancient times. What sort of awful picture, in turn, could the tempter have shown him at that point? What a horde of inconsolable figures in hairy garments, distorted by fanatic mortifications to the point of being feeble shadows, made gloomy by genuflections and prayers about which heart and thought come to know nothing, and to no purpose come to be exerted within a narrow sphere of dead works; and all this would arise without the old version of them already being deadened and short of any joyful life appearing.

If the tempter had also shown him this picture and had pushed at him with the question as to whether he would then want to risk fulfilling his dream even at this price and whether he would not find it more advisable to return again into the concealed life from which he was poised to step forth and in quiet prayers to bring his reputation to bear with his Father alone, whether even his Father would want to ease the fate of his brothers and sisters in some other way. For himself, however, was it not more advisable to leave humankind to itself, to see whether without him it might find a more moderate exit from the darkness that kept it surrounded? In contrast, imagine an individual, even a most courageous one, who does, albeit quite certainly, walk the path of faith for oneself alone, even if evil spirits would have threatened this individual from every rooftop. Imagine a most joyful individual, who is not afraid to demand every possible sacrifice for what is good, not only of oneself but of others as well. We might well ask whether, given such views into the future, each one of the two would not be worn down and would not have withdrawn a hand from the plow.

However, you might perhaps ask: Did the Lord then truly undergo such a temptation, or, at that time, were not these far-off events as yet hidden from him, as he himself says that the Father reserved many a thing to himself alone? Yet, it does become evident, clearly enough, based on his own words, and not only given those of our text but even more based on what follows, how he would rouse son against father and daughter against mother; also, based on other precautionary and reassuring talk, how definitively these images might also have been lodged in his mind. Notice further with what unshakable composure, with what heroic tranquility, he has said all that he has reported! Indeed, he scarcely seemed able to wait for the fire to flame up that he had come to light! Yes, certainly, he did not have to communicate at all after the manner of other benefactors but had to offer more to what is good for human beings than what had been proffered hitherto! Moreover, since he possessed absolutely nothing apart from himself to offer but instead was poorer in external things than anyone, he had to carry what was superhuman within himself, had to be aware of an inexhaustible source of spiritual blessings. Indeed, he would also have had to know that he was the sole possessor of these good things, and that human beings could not attain to any such possession in any other way than through him. Further, this means, in fact, that he would have had to be aware of a divine force and wealth, and in such a way that he would not assign any special weight to it all. Rather, he had to let even this temptation, of which he had withheld any notice from his disciples because they could not yet handle it, slide from him and in this way would enter the path of his calling worthily.

Suppose that with the eye of the spirit one could foresee merely the smallest part of such perplexities and ravages that would result from one's own efforts and that these efforts had been selfish and egotistic, aiming only at personal fame and power. Would we not say then—but what am I asking, for have we not said it a thousand times that this is superhuman? Rather, this person would have to be driven by a stronger, dark force, the same person who was able to do this in cold blood, with a peaceful soul, with undisturbed consciousness. Yet, likewise, if the work of universal redemption and universal salvation, or blessedness, amounts only to stimulating and beatifying human endeavors, if the one who brings a sword in this way first gives oneself up to the power of the sword, and this not at random, and if this person wants nothing but to create among human beings the higher life that is already borne within oneself and to found it on a permanent basis, then we may indeed say that such a plan and design would be simply empty delusion if it were lacking in a higher power. In this fashion, moreover, no one could endure the picture of misery that would have had preceded its realization and accompanied it if a divine power did not dwell within oneself. To be sure, in a divine manner the Lord would have had to be aware that after every entanglement of the sword and under it he could not miss leading the feet of human beings onto the path of peace, a peace that is higher than any peace known to the hitherto existing world. This person would surely have had to know that, after all these destructions; and under the same, he or she would free them from darkness and the shadow of death and would place them into the beauteous realm of light and of love. This person would surely have had to know that all these hostile motions would consist of nothing other than the final battles of the old death, from which he or she was even then redeeming human beings, and the decisive birth pains of new and eternal life, which was just at that point being received in human nature.

However, such confidence and with it a consciousness that the fullness of divinity was dwelling within this person, such that it would be the Father's words and works that he or she was speaking and doing, and it would be the Father's eternal decree and will that was simply being carried out by him or her and that he or she was moving to accomplish. This would be the case, for the confidence that this divine decree was passing through all those horrors could not possibly fail of its goal, and the certainty that this very person was divinely moved to this end and that this will of God was so completely one's own, that the two aspects of the process could never separate, not even in the most dubious element of life. Such an awareness would surely seem to all of us to be completely comprised of one and the same thing, and we could have no Redeemer who would bring a sword in such a striking manner unless he or she were the only-begotten Son [offspring] of the Father and, like the Father, would be full of grace and truth in all things.

My good friends, we are not yet at the end, however, and even in this respect we have not yet completely gotten to the bottom of the word that

Jesus spoke, namely: "I have come to bring a sword," or should it suffice to remember what the witnesses and disciples of the Lord suffered from the enemies of his word?

Oh, in these days, when we especially want to enjoy his coming on earth and thus also his entire work, may we not also shut our eyes against the internal history of the Christian church! Ah, even then and there, at the time in which the sword would have been raging, even there we see fathers and children, brothers and sisters, rise against one another, in the most vehement quarrels as to what is actually the true meaning of blessedness, or salvation, in Christ and as to what the necessary means are, what the essential and indispensable conditions are, for partaking of it.[7]

Did he also know and foresee all this? We may indeed not doubt it! This is so, for even if his gentleness did not express one aspect of the process so clearly as another, when we remember, my good friends, how ardently in his last solemn prayer he implored from his and our heavenly Father precisely that those whom his Father had given to him during his earthly life, as well as those who would have faith in him through their word might be absolutely at one with one another, just as he and the Father are one. This ardent prayer properly reminds us, like the effect of a dim but all too sure presentiment of his divine mind and heart, that it will not always be this way among them. Further, my good friends, just as they are not completely one in Spirit—and they are no longer that way and cannot be that way—as soon as they would be striving for unity other than "the unity of the Spirit in the bond of peace,"[8] ah, they, in turn, would also be exposed to all those disruptions that ever more arise from factions of every kind, from manifold delusions that the magical force of the letter and of mere statutes brings forth. He thus knew even this side of Christian history, which has already been repeated so often under diverse forms. That he also had to bring this sword instead of peace, what would be more suitable for weakening and darkening the pure impression that his work could otherwise make on human beings?

Can there be a greater obstacle to faith for those who, in every period, would not yet have faith than when they would have seen that precisely there, where love is established as the law that is to govern everyone, where inner peace still could be the sole sure compensation for all external adversities—that even there discord would prevail, that even

---

7. In 1824, what comes up here is the reference to the working of doctrinal theology itself, thus all the other workings of this visible church alluded to just below.

8. Eph 4:3 (NRSV).

there animosity would break out, that even there a sword would rage? Yet, so it is. Yet, my good friends, when on the cross the Lord prayed to his Father for his enemies and persecutors and even presented them to his Father as people who did not know what they were doing, ah, in the same way he also contemplated there the large grouping of souls who, since his coming and completion of his life's work, would have fallen into pitiable conflict concerning his work, his teachings, and the structure of his church. Accordingly, he had always known in advance the aberrations of love and of slipping onto the path of discontent among those who had actually wanted to walk on the path of peace. Such people are also not knowing what they are doing. Moreover, even being on the cross did not hinder our Lord and did not halt his steps, so that he could overlook even this familiar pattern with the same equanimity and peace. Indeed, he knew that some of his own followers were like this too and had separated among themselves. Moreover, they too had been embittered against one another externally, with a hostility that an ordinary eye could not differentiate from the resentment of egotistic passions. Yet, they too had already been saved from the darkness and the shadows of death, given with which these groups were already being suffused with light and with which, they would have nothing more to do. Even so, their feet had already been led to the path of peace, because they had been seeking to become at one, under one Lord, one under the same shepherd, even if, out of human blindness, they were fighting this noble spiritual struggle for truth with improper and forbidden weapons.

That he judged even such discontent in this manner and not otherwise is, on the one hand, the clearest proof that he saw matters human exactly as the Father in heaven sees them, the Father to whom he commended his own followers. Yet, on the other hand, we have to admit, nonetheless, that in order to begin and to effect in this manner the work of redemption, a divine self-consciousness was required, even given foresight such as this. By itself, human power would not have been able either to imagine or to execute this self-consciousness. Only the one who, once he knew all this, could act in this manner—the Redeemer, who had also appeared as the one who had come down from on high and was aware of an eternal reign and of a secured dominion by which all of this, in turn, would be made even and equalized, indeed would be transformed into peace and blessedness, or salvation.[9]

9. This entire section amounts to an added reflection within and contemplation upon *Christian Faith*, notably its Division there on "prophetic" doctrine (§§157–63)

III

Yet, precisely for this reason, my good friends, the fact that the Lord could not help bringing a sword is the surest standard for the unshakeable firmness of the union between the Redeemer and his own.

We know how little his work had already advanced when, in turn, he had to leave the earthly scene so quickly that even he himself wished in a human way that the cup that he was to drink might be removed from him,[10] even if only one time. However, even to him at this time, this event on the cross did not seem unexpected. Rather, already when he wanted to begin the work that his Father had directed him to do, this same person who knew what was within a human being had to be resigned to executing what was the greatest act with weak instruments. Further, in order not to remember, not only that even the disciple who betrayed him was among the twelve disciples, but also that the rest who had also been working with him had asked, Lord, is it I? See, they were weak instruments, even when he had to leave them. The ones whom he had gathered around himself as his dearest and most intimate followers were weak and were altogether still remaining weak. May people now take a look simply at their execution of the Lord's instructions, for recently they had still been talking among themselves as to who should be the next one in heaven after the Master. May people then also take a look at the proper conception of his purpose and at what would count as mature insight into his teaching, for, at the same time, they were still imagining an external glory in which he would eventually reveal himself. Furthermore, even later on, many among those Christians who adhered to the external rites of Judaism found some support. Thus, in every respect they were still children regarding faith, just like the Christians about whom the apostle says: They could not yet tolerate strong food; rather, they still had to be nourished with the first milk of the gospel. Further, now they were supposed to start nourishing others immediately. Indeed, from then on the entire success of his mission rested on their witness and on their proclamation, for, to be sure, Christ alone accomplished the work of reconciliation and justification of humankind in its humble relation to

and grounded in the second half of Division Two (§§148–56). Continuing in this third thematic section of the sermon, Schleiermacher was also constructing a corresponding picture of what happened on the cross, one alternative to most traditional theories of the atonement.

10. Matt 26:39.

God. For this activity, not only did he not need anyone to help him, but he also could not use anyone to accomplish it. However, if now human beings were also to rejoice in this work, not only did he himself actually have to appear, but even after him the gospel actually had to be preached and union among Christians had to be established. Correspondingly, the apostle Paul directly juxtaposes the following two features: praising God for being in Christ and reconciling the world to God and for founding the ministry of his followers, which itself proclaims the message of reconciliation among human beings.[11] Yet, which apostles would have been appropriate for giving such a message, using whatever means would serve such a purpose, if they had remained as they were at that time! How would it have been possible that, even if among myriad deficiencies, everything that subsequent ages saw being developed in the strength that comes of having faith, in purity of insight, in confidence amid dangers, in steadfastness amid temptations, in the power of love, and in joyfulness of hope within the Christian church would actually have proceeded from them! Moreover, as soon as the Redeemer himself was removed from this earthly life, there were no means for affecting human beings other that through these same disciples, who could, however, bring forth in others nothing but what they themselves had.

Yet, also hear how they came to be who they were. Hear it from the mouth of one of the apostles himself [Paul], namely: We endure persecution, but we are not abandoned; we have affliction, but we are not afraid; we are suppressed, but we do not perish; we bear the dying of Christ in our body at all times, so that the life of the Lord also comes to be known in us.[12] Thus, as he also said: What can separate us from the love of God? Affliction, or fear, or persecution, or hunger, or nakedness, or danger from a sword? In all that, we do greatly overcome, for we know that no force, either earthly or unearthly, nor any distinction between life and death, can ever separate us from the love of God, which is in Christ Jesus.[13]

Yet, what does this same apostle also say in such letters to early Christian comrades? He says that we greatly overcome for the sake of the one who loved us. Moreover, what does he place foremost in these letters? He says: This abundant power is God's and is not from us![14] That power

11. 2 Cor 5:19, 20.

12. 2 Cor 4:8, 9.

13. Rom 8:35–39.

14. 2 Cor 4:7.

has come from Christ, who was of God, and it was Christ's life that was made known in this manner. The Lord himself had to know this when he came to bring a sword and, first in an earthly manner, had to sink under its force himself. He had to know that after the divine force that dwelt within him, once it had just begun its efficacious action by his coming to the earth, it would continuously have to be active and to perform ever greater works. He had to know that he would remain among his own forever, that their understanding of him would be transfigured ever more, that their love toward him would be purified ever more, and that in this way they would come to be fit for conveying his message without his bodily presence but yet only by virtue of his spiritual presence. Through their passing denial, and through their recurrent inconstancy, he would have had to see that he was in a position to ignite in all minds and hearts of persons of faith a love and a faithfulness like that of Stephen, that first martyr whose memory is commemorated on this very day. This martyr, who, when in the face of death, testified that in Jesus of Nazareth all promises given to the fathers are fulfilled and in him alone blessedness, or salvation, for all is to be found, did not see the rage of the excited crowd, the stones that were already being raised to smash his brightly illuminated and fervent head to pieces. He saw nothing of all these hostile motions but saw only heaven, to which his change of life had been opened already here on earth, and he saw the Son of Man standing at the right hand of God.[15] Accordingly, the firm inner conviction, which he had just pronounced and for the sake of which he, at that point, so little honored continuation of his earthly life that it might have materialized on to some bright conception. Instead, what he did was to shed his life like a fruitful grain of wheat that does not remain alone when it dies but keeps itself unto eternal life and still brings forth much fruit.[16]

Yes, my good friends, the Lord's confidence had to be in the Lord himself, so that in this way, and ever more magnificently, he would continue to live among his own, and this confidence also refers to us as surely as he even now continues to be effectual[17] and also has only us, the whole body of Christians living in every period, through whom he then works. Thus is our first main Christian festival attached to the last one regarding

15. Acts 7:55.

16. John 12:24, 25.

17. In Schleiermacher's 1826/27 lectures on *Christliche Sittenlehre* [*Christian Ethics*] (ed. Peiter, 2011), "to be effectual," "effective" or "efficacious" in one's action is the primary term used (*wirkend, wirksam*).

the Redeemer's life on earth. How could we too truly rejoice in the coming of the Redeemer if we could not also be glad that the same force of love and of faithfulness and of everything that the apostle designates as the fruit of the Spirit were not poured out over us as well and by the same Spirit? If we welcome Christ as our Lord in these festive days, that too can happen only by the Holy Spirit, which is the source of all these gifts.[18] If we welcome Christ as the one who frees us from all other modes of binding, this can only be and continue to be the truth, if, at the same time, by the indissoluble binding of love he holds us firmly joined with himself to one life, just as he has also promised that when he would be raised from the earth, he would want to draw everyone to himself. Now, if we too are subjects of this confidence that Christ had, the confidence that all human life is to become one with his life, then this confidence, as surely as it belongs to the divinity of his being, must also come to be our portion, and we too must be effectual in this confidence. Hence, if even we—although neither placed at the beginnings of the Christian church nor living at its outskirts, also experience in many a sense that we too must bring a sword but only in the way he did. That is, our way too lies not in our merely taking up the sword and drawing it ourselves, as it were, so that we do not perish by that method but if we must bring a sword, then let us be of good cheer, always holding fast, as he did, to that liberating love which can always view even those who still oppose his truth as individuals who do not know what they are doing.

In contrast, then, permeated by his love, let us all the more gladly merge all our powers into the salutary service of making him known to those who out of ignorance are in some manner still against the Lord. Indeed, let us do this in such a way that with each individual we, for our part, are intent on peace but also in such a way that we do not abandon the Word of God that is entrusted to us, with the result that, in this way as well, the ministry that teaches reconciliation and that is our collective calling is not drawn into a state of faintheartedness by us and thereby falls into disregard. Suppose, moreover, that in pursuing this calling we are unable to elude quarreling, be it with those who oppose the reign of God out of misunderstanding or with those who, based on the spite of a foolish heart, do not want to be reproved into piety by salutary teaching even though they do acknowledge it. Let us remember, then, that already at the festival of his birth, thus from the very onset of his life, we would

---

18. 1 Cor 12:3.

greet the Redeemer as the Prince of Peace. Let me also recall that he too has always remained this Prince of Peace under each struggle that he himself has waged, with the result that in this sense too his life might continue within us. Further, let us likewise exercise remembrance, both in the midst of internal discord that unfortunately and not infrequently prevails among the confessors of his name, as well as in the midst of external struggle with the world, always to maintain the serene tranquility that was never dulled for him and always in order to tread on the paths of peace. As a result, regardless of the sword, may this peace hold sway on earth, nonetheless, because this peaceableness has taken up its place in the innermost minds and hearts of all persons of faith, and, regardless of all apparent vicissitude, peacefulness shall be found among all human beings to whom the grace of God in Christ has appeared, and who have cast a glance into the depth of riches that reside in the wisdom and knowledge of God. That is to say, because they know that, however often this state of mind and heart might again threaten to become dark around us, the reign of light is firmly grounded, and each matter must serve the community of those whom God loves in God's Son, arising for what is good.

Accordingly, in truth, and irrespective of the sword that our Lord brought, by the one whose birth we celebrate, peace and pleasure have indeed stayed with us, for which may honor then be to God on high, now and forever. Amen.

8

The Very First Appearance of the Redeemer as Proclamation of a Joy that Awaits All Human Beings

The First Day of Christmas
Sunday, December 25, 1831[1]

But the angel said to them, "Do not be afraid; for see—I am bringing you good news of great joy for all the people: to you is born this day in the city of David a Savior, who is the Messiah [Christ], the Lord."

—LUKE 2:10–11 (NRSV)

So, my devout friends, the coming of the Redeemer on earth was proclaimed as a joy, which would befall all people. Thus, the thoughts of those to whom this proclamation happened were immediately and fully directed toward the future. To be sure, it was not a proclamation of some one thing in the future, a proclamation that is based on nothing further and intends somehow to establish itself alone. Rather, it referred to something that had already happened. This is so, for it is said: "To you is born

1. This sermon was taken down at the main morning service by a parishioner "almost word-perfect," then "slightly revised" by Schleiermacher with a view to its being read. It was first published in a local, limited edition (1832), 38–54; then in SW II.2 (1835), 132–42; and (1843), 137–47 (the text for this translation). The most recent subsequent edition is that in KGA III.12 (2013), 823–33. It was followed by another sermon the next day, December 26, at the same hour, the main service; that sermon is also included in the present volume.

this day in the city of David a Savior, who is Christ, the Lord." However, the blessing, or salvation, that was to proceed from the newborn child was indeed presented to them not as something merely current but as a "joy for all the people" occurring only within the future. Moreover, to be sure, if it was to be a savior who was born to them, if blessing, or salvation, was to be accomplished through him, then they could not already have it if it were viewed as something current, and they could not rejoice in it if his birth were to be announced at that time only. So, it is just like this among us, my devout friends.

Suppose that in these holy days we visualize in the light of this world certain elements of the Lord's birth, notably the humble scene of his first appearance. In that scene would we strive in vain to catch sight of the blessing, or salvation, of the world, the light that was yet to penetrate into the darkness. In vain we would strive to observe in the child the divine form of him who did not consider being equal to God to be plundered.[2] It would also be in vain if we should strive to observe in the weak, needy infant the one whose power, in turn, was to raise up humankind from the abyss into which it had sunk through its many faults. Because the Lord's birth offers so little that is current, only later in the Christian church's history was its observance also set, and there are still many communities of Christians who do not celebrate his birth because their faith, their trust, is based on what is being accomplished for them and for us but is not based on the one who is born to be the very light of this world.

My dear friends, the faith that I always assume among those to whom I speak in this place where we may enjoy mutual edification includes, to be sure, a recognition that the divine power by which Jesus could come to be the Savior of the world was itself not united with the man Jesus at some later point in time. As a result, we may not separate him from God in some dubious fashion. This is the case, because if he had been only a human child as we are, without bearing the divine Word within himself, unavoidably he would also have to have partaken in sin just as we do. Our faith accepts this being human as we are about him when we think back to his first appearance on earth. However, we might well be unable to see this difference in the child Jesus, and in his first appearance we would look around in vain for anything that would have made known this great and immeasurable difference from all other human beings. Yet, if already at that early moment when he appeared on

2. Or "exploited" (NRSV), as in sheer, brazen robbery (Phil 2:6), in contrast to his humble status as a human being.

earth devotion at the Redeemer's cradle was, nevertheless, conducted in such an extraordinary manner as our narrative states, why then, should our own devotion not also think back to that time and to those actual circumstances of his first appearance? For this reason, then, the celebration of his birth also gradually became almost universal in the Lord's church. To be sure, it became so only when all reliable transmission concerning the time of year when the Redeemer actually saw that the light of the world had already been lost, and that in effect only so much had been left to us, that we could know the following, namely, that in determining the time of our festival a law would have been observed other than the meager probability that results from the external circumstances given to us. All the more so is this special law also a sign to us that when we celebrate this festival we must not stay with what had already happened at the time of our Lord's birth but must look at what, at that same time, was yet to occur in the future. However, precisely what was actually still to occur in the future, what a long past it had already been for us humans, and now what a present is yet to be placed before us! How many hearts of human beings has the Redeemer of the world already gained for himself? In how many tongues is his splendor recognized? For how many people has he not already become the law and regulator of their entire life! However, is the present itself, as it were, the point at which our attention may remain? Has the Redeemer's divine being—as he indeed came to make himself known to us and in particular to sacrifice himself for us to that end—already merged into the entirety of humankind, indeed completely and perfectly so, and yet merged only into a single human soul? Has the light already permeated the darkness completely and entirely and thus dispersed the darkness, or must we not admit that even now, if we want to behold him in his splendor, we may not stick with what is present but must direct our glance into the future?

Accordingly, in harmony with the guidance that lies in the words of our text, let us then consider precisely the first appearance of the Redeemer as the proclamation of a joy that has drawn nigh for all human beings! What we want warmly to recommend to ourselves, in this respect, is twofold. First, that this joy in the appearance of the Redeemer comprises the true prototype for each and every joy that we might have in the future, but then, second, that this faith is also one that grasps hold of this future joy, one that is and grants our sole surety with respect to each and every concern that we can have regarding the future.

I

Thus, in the first place, my dear friends, this joy in the future, which was to begin with the appearance of the Lord but was still not at all visible at his birth, is the prototype of each and every joy that we can have in the future. Accustomed as all of us often are, to direct our glance beyond what is present, well into the future. Nonetheless, the richer we are in such experience, the more surely can we also come to a place wherein each and every such joy is present, this in accordance with its nature, which is also something quite indeterminate. The joy that could be stirred by the call of the angel among those who heard the angel's words will also have been like this at our own particular time. It is a joy, says the angel, that shall be for all people throughout the world! Now, did not their notions concerning what was to unfold from this child's birth also have to be restricted to their own people at that time, whereas everything else lacking illumination by the radiance of this joy, was dimly to recede into a dark distance? If they were reminded that he was born to them "in the city of David," that he is a "lord" within that city, did not their sight have to be directed backward into the past, so that they could consider more closely that glorious figure David from the time of their ancestors? Did they not have to imagine a similarity between that ancient king of their people and the one who was born to them now as their future Lord? Thus, the more they took hold of these words, the more easily they would have been mistaken in many aspects of the birth announcement. How little would they have grasped the truth! How readily each image that they could fashion based on these words would have represented something other than what actually came into existence afterward!

A joy that shall be "for all the people" was proclaimed to them. Ah, even up to this very hour it has not actually been for all the people of whom the angel of the Lord had spoken there. A large part of this people is still turned away from the blessing, or salvation, the vision of which had also appeared to the shepherds in their beholding this child. Yet, how many other peoples have discovered this light, in addition to them; have warmed themselves in it; and by it have been wakened to the higher life about which the shepherds could not create even the slightest notion from the angel's words! Thus, as this piece of writing assures us, a time will also come when all Israel will attain to blessing, or salvation. None of this exists, however, except that which is offered to human beings in the one name, and even now this eventual time is still a future time. Thus, if the shepherds heeded the words of the proclamation, how little could they properly and surely consider, with respect to this point of the divine decrees,[3] the actual order of events in time. So, we find that this is characteristic of all the prophecies of which the books of the Old Testament are full; it is also the case with the few prophecies that we find in the books of the New Testament. Moreover, the sagacity of those who attempted to interpret them always strove in vain to explicate for themselves and for others a definite picture of what was intended in the prophecies given.

Accordingly, my good friends, this is also the case with us! When, given the Redeemer's appearance, we think of the joy that shall still exist for us, likewise we must also be resigned to the fact that our depictions of the future—however glorious they would surely be in relation to Christ, however clearly and brightly his divine power would be revealed in it all—are indeed also nothing but images assembled from such indefinite notions. Thereby we are able sooner to represent the very last thing among them with some well-defined clarity.

Suppose that we ask the following questions: What is the accomplishment of Christ's blessing, or salvation? When will one flock exist as if there were only one shepherd? When will the community of the Lord be represented in the entire diversity of the future flock's composition and in the full spread of its extent, given that it is described for us as a living whole,[4] as his spiritual body on earth, everything in it reigned over by the Spirit, which he will have poured out, all in contrast from flesh's being overcome, everyone having grown to the point of similarity with the consummate age reached by Christ? Of these conditions I say we can form a definite likeness more soon than not, at least in their general features. This is so, for should we indeed add all these conditions, viewed as happily done away with and overcome, to what still holds us back, away from that perfection which Christ had, what would still hamper and oppress us? In a word, if, at the same time, we should definitively realize our distinction from that perfection, then we would indeed also have to permeate the entire present in order to accomplish an image of the future in this way. Based on this consideration, moreover, it already follows that if we were to survey all the major intermediary points, if we

---

3. See items from *Christian Faith* (2016) in the "one eternal divine *decree*" in its Analytical Index.

4. See items related to "church," "community" and "whole" in the Analytical Index of *Christian Faith* (2016).

were to search into the further development of the divine decrees[5] up to this goal of perfection, or consummate completeness, if we should want to know what kind of struggles will still exist to be endured, how much of that which, even if it does not seem to exist in its perfection, might nonetheless, at least in terms of its overall tendency, now seem to correspond to that final, complete image—yet, in turn, this will be repressed by the oft recurring force of flesh and of sin.[6] Suppose that we should want to know wherefrom a light will first come to pass for those who still dwell in the shadow of death. Suppose that we should want to know in what way the many conflicting voices that we now hear so often among those who do indeed profess one Lord will be compiled with each ensuing difference coming from peace, harmony, and a melodious sound worthy of the Lord. We are not able to imagine this state any more than those shepherds could imagine in what way the newborn child would fulfill what was promised of him.

One could ask, however, if the uncertainty that is necessarily attached to our joy in the future is so great, does this joy not then lose its entire value for us? To be sure, my dear friends, something does belong to this future, such that this joy does have some value for us. Moreover, we may not conceal it from ourselves: Everything that we are able to envision in the future, everything that can be communicated and proclaimed to us about this future cannot but achieve truth for us, for it simply belongs to the goods of our life if it is in accord with our inner longing, if it satisfies the tendency of our own minds and hearts and in this way brings us to a state of peace.[7] We do not know to what extent the shepherds who heard the proclamation of the angel were themselves among those who awaited the blessing, or salvation, proclaimed in the prophecies of the Old Testament and gladly turned from the oppressive present to an imagined finer and freer future. The narrative, from which the words of our text are taken, gives us no account of this turn. To be sure, the shepherds did not disdain the proclamation, but when the heavenly host had disappeared they said, we want to go to Bethlehem and witness the story

---

5. Ordinarily God's one "decree" is not plural for Schleiermacher. Here the plural denotes aspects or iterations of one divine decree, wholly self-consistent and eternal.

6. See "flesh" in the Analytical Index of *Christian Faith* (2016). As in Paul's writings "flesh" is generally used in contrast to "spirit," and "sin" is used in contrast to "grace."

7. See reference to "peace" as a state in *Christian Faith* (2016), Analytical Index—one for both individuals and communities.

they proclaimed to us, and when they found it to be so, they continued to spread the word.

Yet, whether for themselves the experience remained a truth guiding their life, whether it moved them to follow the child further in the unfolding of his life, the child who was then so insignificant, whether they belonged among the disciples of the Lord—we know nothing about any of this. How easily possible it is that for them this proclamation had simply happened without reference to their own situation, had simply happened so that they would come to be bearers of a rumor that was then no longer to disappear, namely, that at last the awaited Messiah had appeared.

In contrast, in other narratives from the early lifetime of our Redeemer we find a more distinct and finer image. That old man, Simeon,[8] who saw the Redeemer in this infant when his mother and Joseph presented him in the temple so as to offer, at the same time, the obligatory offering to Supreme Being, he was certainly one of those who was waiting for the salvation of Israel. To the question, to the burning wish of his heart, a proclamation had happened to him that he still was to see the Savior of the world, and his soul now got so full that he had received enough for the rest of his life, notwithstanding that he had seen his Redeemer only in his childlike imperfection, having no sign of the divine dignity that the young Redeemer bore. However, precisely because this proclamation coincided with the inner longing of the old man's heart, for him it was a reason for and a cause of peace, and he knew that now the Lord would and could do nothing but let him, his servant, travel in this state of peace. Moreover, the same thing held true of the prophetess Anna, who by chance was present at that time, and who, in accordance with her hopes and out of the fullness of need and her own faith, now became a bearer of this proclamation, itself probably totally different from that of the shepherds.

So, my dear friends, among us as well, this is how our situation is now. Can we all not do anything but admit that, in comparison with what is yet to arise, the present is indeed still as incomplete as the human appearance of the Redeemer was at that time when his eye first opened to earthly light? In a thousand different ways, we ourselves are driven to look out into the future. The proper joy in the future as it will evolve from and by this blessing, or salvation, in Christ is possessed only by those

8. Luke 2:25–38.

who themselves bear a heartfelt longing for the peace that they do not know how to attain based on their own power alone. This is the case, for it is true that spiritual perfection and fullness is something that they must indeed imagine as the goal of their striving, though they cannot yet know that they never can achieve it completely on their own. For this reason, the Redeemer always rightly said that he came simply to be a healer of the sick. Each word of consolation, each invitation that he expressed—indeed each of these invitations always came to pass—especially if insofar as it was truly grasped and became truth in a human soul—was simply a presentiment of the further development that was reserved for the future. As such, moreover, each consolation or invitation could become a living truth only in its reception, but that also means reception within needy minds and hearts. For this reason, the Redeemer so often lamented how overly clever those among whom he lived also were with respect to earthly matters, how much they had practiced in this earthly domain also to the point of their exploring the future based on a perception taken from present experience and moved onward, yet they did not understand the true signs of the times regarding heavenly life. Hence, in the world it is such a common complaint, raised ever and again throughout their earthly life and at each great turning point of human affairs, in each moment that bears struggle over great things, namely in that, given each and every sign of the future that the present offers, all knowledge, like that focused on what is present, has arisen from the past. In short, not every experience makes human beings learned regarding what will evolve from the present. Rather, all too often human beings act nonetheless in such a way that what they wish least is what must ensue. If our minds and hearts take a direction different from that borne by divine wisdom, if we desire something other than what God has ordained in God's eternal decree,[9]

9. The theme that is further clarified and explained in this 1831 sermon lies in the affirmation that the final goal, or end, of the one eternal divine decree is contained in the concept "peace." Earlier in this sermon the *one decree* of creation and redemption ("new creation") is closely adjoined to "love" and "joy," thus is introduced as "decrees." Here, consider his masterful 1819 essay *On the Doctrine of Election* (ET: Nicol and Jorgenson, 2012), which was issued in preparation for the first edition of *Christian Faith* (1821–1822) and in order to resolve a key issue historically dividing Reformed and Lutheran theologians in Germany. Many of their corresponding churches did unite in 1821, his own already "dual" congregation at Berlin's Dreifaltigkeitskirche being the first among them. The doctrinal treatment presented in the second edition of *Christian Faith* (1830–1831; ET: Tice et al., 2016) is also consistent with the historically examined doctrine given in the essay.

then it is also not possible for us to pursue traces of the future in the present. Instead, by the inclination of our own hearts alone we are bound to be led astray. Moreover, what is thus right and true, as well as beneficial joy in the future, can be had only by those who desire only that the divine decree of love be realized, who seek only that pure blessedness, or salvation, which Christ has brought to all human beings, and who strive only for the peace of human beings with God. This peace finds its sole guarantee in the accomplishment of God's divine work.

II

Second, my devout friends, let us now consider how, on the other hand, still today, even this joy of our festival, the joy that is turned out into the future, also solely grants to us surety and confidence regarding each and every concern that we could have with respect to the future, precisely because it is based on what has already happened.

Now, hereby, to be sure, we must first consider that this entire experience of interconnectedness is always simply a matter of faith, in that even what at that earlier time had already occurred could be grasped only with faith, so that even the consolation that we can have regarding the future is based only on faith.[10] What did the angel say to the shepherds

---

In *Christian Faith*, Part Two, Second Aspect, its Division Two, matters regarding "The Emergence of the Church" (§§113–25), comprised of the doctrines of election and predestination, are initiated by "Communication of the Holy Spirit." The two sets of doctrines are considered to be inextricably combined. They immediately follow treatments of grace in Christ, regeneration, conversion, justification and sanctification, and they are followed by two Divisions on the "Continuation" and "Consummation" of the church, respectively. Finally, the entirely organic, closely interconnected organization of the work is itself capped by an examination and necessarily provisional explication of a doctrine featuring "The Triune God." The latter, the work's conclusion, lies implicit within the entire systematic presentation of doctrines. This feature shows up with sharpest clarity in Part Two, most proleptically in Part One, and preparatively in the Introduction, withal consistently step by step. By announced intention, then, this organism is fed by every department and discipline of theological work. See *Brief Outline* (1811, 1830; ET: Tice, 2011), §§1–8ff.

Hence, he intends theological documents to be rough guidelines to activities rooted in proclamation of the gospel, as is preaching itself, not to be literally determinative, as if they were impermeable legal prescriptions. On this account, we are to expect further light from sermons like this one and those that follow (1832, 1833) in the present volume of sermons.

10. This sentence too points to a theme that builds on *Christian Faith*. It too offers an inner–outer scaffold of relations between past, present, and future. In addition, it

following the words of the angel's proclamation, which we have read? This is the sign that the angel indicated: "You will find the child wrapped in swaddling clothes and lying in a manger." What a sign! On that basis, how could they have grasped even a mere presentiment of a joy that shall be "to all people"! Is this a splendid sign for the Savior, who is Christ the Lord, being born today? Yes, if the extraordinary appearance that had already occurred previously had not disposed the minds and hearts of these shepherds to a faithful confidence, namely, that one human being was born who does not come without a higher providence,[11] this sign would sooner have made them disinclined to believe the word of proclamation than that it would have strengthened them in it. This is how it was from the beginning on and always will be. In the figure of the Redeemer only faith could hold firm the joy that was not only to all people but to the entirety of humankind as well.

What would a lack of faith still have to say even at the time when the Lord had already appeared and taught, when he already walked about and performed miracles, when the people there were already adhering to him in great numbers and were crowding around him? Would any high official have had faith in him? Was it not said: Can anything good come out of Galilee? Has a prophet ever appeared from there? Accordingly, the wish of the heart would then have been guided falsely, the signs that Supreme Being[12] gave would have been misunderstood, a lack of faith

---

makes clearer, in this respect, that as a matter of faith internally necessary, enabled and developed, Christian faith can harvest an overall worldview. In his time and place, and in company with his quite socially diverse parishioners, the terms of this discourse would have to have become an amalgam comparable to the contemporary but timelessly intricate religious upsweep of Bach, the nicely regulated sounds and rhythms of Haydn, and the lively articulated even brashly revolutionary musical narratives of Beethoven's later works from about 1808 on.

In the third characteristic Schleiermacher's mode of thought would be totally "modern" and, more than ever, organically interconnected. Here, in sermonic form, one sees Schleiermacher mopping up something of what is left over from the careful analytical and scientific ("didactical-dialectic") infrastructures used in *Christian Faith*, adding to these the Romantic rhetorical and poetic styles for delivering content used in the sermons.

11. See Index below for instances of this term, which goes with his conception of divine election but brings problems of its own (regarding God's supposed literal "foreseeing") and so does not describe a separable locus of doctrine for him.

12. You may have noted that in this translation "Supreme Being" never has a "the" before it. The reason is that Schleiermacher uses this term for God *in se*, thus not for a singular being but for that which is above and beyond all being, for the unknowable

would have been unable to grasp the future based on what it saw. Hence, subsequently even the apostles of the Lord repeatedly had to revert to the fact that Christ's teaching, the proclamation of his blessings, or salvation, was foolishness for some and an offense to others, because they lacked the inner faith with which they could grasp the future in the present.

Suppose, however, that the shepherds had held firm the faith that had been awakened in them; oh then they would indeed have said, even given what soon happened in Bethlehem, that, nonetheless, the baby boy will surely be glad to elude the great destiny foretold, and he will not have been affected by the murderous snake. Moreover, given each and every anxiety of the age, they would have thought: The one born in the city of David is to be our royal Lord, and he will protect us against all this! Further, if they should come to feel depressed by the burden of the law, they would have consoled themselves with the fact that the Savior was born, who, in one way or another, will ever take this burden from his people. To be sure, Simeon and Anna were happy in having such faith during that probably rather short time of their long pilgrimage, though they saw and heard nothing more of this child of promise, and their continuously holding fast to this same joyfulness is far more applicable to all of us.

Suppose, on the other hand, that we have repeatedly been troubled, because we have seen that not all evil is yet overcome by what is good, but we also see that much of what we have hoped for has repeatedly been hampered in its efficacy, and we see that the powers of human beings, for all of whom the same provision from on high has happened, and who externally belong to the same community composed of persons of faith, joined so little in order to advance together that to which they profess to be their highest wish—yes, do suppose that in these ways our joy in the future would come to be saddened, again and again. Then, the sole basis for all this would always bear the same characteristic, namely a lack of faith.

Suppose that we had once come to be steadfast in the proper Christmas joy, that the Savior had been born for us and we would have no other savior to expect. Then, indeed, nothing that could happen could allow us to be discouraged about the future, as he himself proclaimed it and to which, if we ask ourselves, the inner voice of our hearts does testify. Yes,

---

God beyond God who inspires human beings and reveals Godself in human history as Father (Progenitor, Author), Son, and Holy Spirit, as in a communal and personal relationship with humankind.

suppose that, in a way proper to persons of faith, we were to search within our souls and observe ourselves in the complex web of our thoughts and sentiments. Suppose too that we would bring to mind and compare the better elements of our life for which we would thank God, and suppose that given those elements, we would gladly bury them into oblivion if we did not know that their memory serves to augment our betterment, but of which we would, nevertheless, have to be ashamed. Would we ever be able to bear any witness other than this: How else would that for which we would thank and praise God always be simply that which we have done in the Lord's name, whereby he was present to us, so that driven to him by love, and despising of everything else, we would have found our entire well-being solely in him and in the endeavor to serve him and to follow him? This experience, which is always repeated in any significant relationship, which each person confirms to another as to how one has the experience in itself, proves its worth at the same time. It does so as the key to everything that will have happened from the time when the Redeemer of the world appeared on earth to this very day, and that now gives us a secure guarantee—a guarantee in regard not only to what may still be in store for us but also in regard to what lies far beyond our earthly existence! We would instantly attend to the fact that this measure will always be valid. Everything that wants to separate from him and exist without him, however much it may glitter, must pass away. In contrast, on the proclamation of his name, on the union between persons of faith that he founded, on the teaching of the cross that will never cease to be proclaimed where his name is mentioned—on these things alone is based the trust that drives away each and every fear of the future.

Accordingly, my dear friends, let us then look out into the future with a joyful eye, by truly assembling at the very first beginning of the life of our Redeemer. To be sure, after we have held the image of perfection before ourselves, we will all gladly admit that as it lies before us now, the reign of God has not yet grown much farther than in the days of his child-hood. Far from being perfect human beings similar to Christ, humankind is scarcely more developed than a child who has become powerful over oneself only to such an extent that the child now says "I" and has thereby barely discovered oneself. Indeed, humankind has scarcely developed so far, for how otherwise did the voices of Christians allow themselves to be scattered about so widely, how did almost every little band of a few persons come to believe itself to be the reign of God and for itself alone!

If it had actually grown to such an extent, how it is that all persons, within the entire sphere of those professing faith in the Redeemer, would always have to think as one among themselves? In contrast, how could each small band have to think of itself simply as a single part that exists only within one great whole, only by virtue of it, only for it? Thus, how much of our community would also still have to become different from what it is, how much would exist within it that still seems to waver, thus has yet to become strong? How much that is scattered, withal in quite diverse directions, would still have to become united?

This set of issues cannot disturb us, for how often does the history of the Christian church not show us similar changes already in these very beginnings? Thus, we too still do not know how many generations of human beings will pass away, how many nations will follow nations, before the light from above, which is given to us, will have illuminated the entire world! In that matter, how many human beings will still leave the scene of this life before those grow up, of whom one may say that the heavenly light has completely permeated their darkness? Indeed, would there be even one single human being about whom one could say that that individual has come to be now completely lit up because one's eye has become wholly full of light? Nevertheless, we want to see into the future with a gladsome glance on this very day, for the work of the Redeemer can neither perish nor even stop short but remains in an uninterrupted process of development. The entire fullness of heavenly light must be shed ever and again on generations of human beings, based on what these eyes of the Redeemer saw, these eyes which at the time of his birth first opened to earthly life. All divine blessings have to come upon human beings from these very hands of the Redeemer, which at that time of beginning could beckon and proclaim simply in instinctive motions a life that did not yet understand itself. Moreover, everything that is true wisdom for those who are of his own kind would have to issue from these lips, which at that time could not even smile. Further, everything that is to be established as a true good, and that we could enjoy in surety and peace, would have to be an utterance by these very lips.

Yes, today we speak of Jesus Christ, he alone, at that time a baby and afterwards in the fullness of his life, yesterday and today, now and in eternity, the same person. Amen.

🌿

Editor's Postscript

Schleiermacher's latest German biographer, Kurt Nowak (2001) reports that in the 1820s he was able to publish "no great work," notably between the two editions of his original edition (1821–1822) and much revised second edition of *Christian Faith* (1830–1831). Yet, on the same page Nowak also indicates that this entire period, right up to his death on February 14, 1834, was "an abundant and stirring" one.[13] Thence he emphasizes the "internal and external obstacles" that got in the way. My disagreement with his judgments probably lies in a different meaning assigned to the phrase "great work" (*grosses Werk*). That is to say, even in the evidence Nowak displays in the final section of his account up to Schleiermacher's death (on pages 389–456) would seem to belie the obvious fertility and efficacy of Schleiermacher's activities that his life showed during the 1820s (1820–1829), even before issuance of his widely reputed greatest work (1830–1831) and not ceasing over the following period (1830–1833). That work, in its essence, is clearly to be described in terms that acknowledge the labor, skill, and spirit that he put into it, not the bound copy of it alone. In that sense, he had actually continued to provide astonishingly numerous and amazing outputs (works), even in the face of considerable external obstacles and overt restraints placed on his path, and despite his occasional reports of "tiredness" or "fatigue" that he might have made to his correspondents during the 1820s. Who wouldn't get rather tired, given the very heavy load that he was carrying particularly during his fifties and early sixties! This would not betoken any real cessation of activities anywhere in his professional, family, or private life even if it might be thought, as Nowak indicates, that he "sought relief" from certain limited administrative duties in 1828. In short, Nowak's account tends to present the period up to Schleiermacher's death as the last two of four phases. The phases run as follows: (1) formative years (1768–1796), (2) experience as a preacher, writer and professor at Halle (1796–1807), (3) the "elevated" (*Höhe*) period (1807–1822), and (4) the greatly troubled, oppressed "final decade" (1823–1834).

What would count as a true "work," then, would be whatever amounts, nevertheless, to any noteworthy example of what labor, skill,

13. Nowak, *Schleiermacher* (2001), 378.

and spirit he would have put into something accomplished. Although Schleiermacher did seek ways to reduce his workload, the chief attempts met with decisive opposition by colleagues or by men holding official power over him, as Nowak himself notes. Here I would simply indicate that Schleiermacher continued all his former activities in the Dreifaltig-keitskirche and at the University of Berlin, where he continued to pile up manuscripts later to be published in his early *Collected Works* (SW: *Sammtliche Werke*) and later in the currently ongoing *Collected Critical Edition* (KGA: *Kritische Gesamtausgabe*) of all that he left behind; the critical edition includes correspondence, occasional essays, and speeches at Berlin's Academy of Sciences (only one each year from 1824 to 1827 during the last two periods, and chiefly on pre-Socratic philosophers and on ethics) or elsewhere, sermons, and subject-oriented volumes of texts in philosophy and theology. All of the material in the KGA is to be regarded as "works," to my mind, and they all tend to be organically interrelated products of his extraordinary, often epoch-making career. He did not stop during this final decade of his life, nor did his reception and influence cease in almost any area of inquiry he touched, despite continual opposition addressed to his publications, at each step seriously contributing to lasting faulty understandings. I do not include his sing-ing tenor and other involvements in the Berliner *Singakademie* (choral society) or his sizeable activity in producing a new *Berliner Gesangbuch* (hymnbook, 1828–30), or other more nearly private pursuits and family trips.

So, any purveyor of information concerning his influence and re-ception is bound to find it difficult to form clear distinctions between his "great" works and those that would be merely contributive to un-derstanding them, and those found to be important in their own right. For example, Schleiermacher's published works that belong to the 1820s would include his *Christian Household* sermons (1820); his annual lengthy exegesis lecture courses, usually on several New Testament books each time (sadly, not yet available in German or English); his series of early Sunday morning or afternoon expository (running interpretation) sermons on Acts (1820), on Particular Gospel Passages (1821), on Philip-pians (1822), and on John (1823–1825); his quite valuable initial two col-lections of select *Christliche Festpredigten* (sermons from special festivals celebrated during past church years) (1826, 1833); his contributions in 1827 and in other years opposing the king's proposed liturgical agenda (1814–1834) for so-called Evangelical (that is, Lutheran and Reformed) churches; and lectures over the years—in addition to his remarks at the grave of his son Nathanael (1829), a piece that gained prominence among his contributions to progressive educational theory and practice in Germany well into the twentieth century and perhaps beyond. The remarks about his son simply comprise a small but poignant part of his various long-term contributions, including those to hermeneutics, the critical arts, aesthetics, politics, ethics, and other sociocultural matters; much of this body of work was not published until after (even far after) his death, or has yet to be published.

The short-lived three issues of the *Theologische Zeitschrift* periodical, founded by DeWette, Lücke, and himself, appeared then (1819–1822), as did two writings associated with the uniting of his Lutheran-Reformed congregation (1820–1821). Further, a greatly enlarged third edition of his discourses *On Religion* appeared in 1821, with endnote references to *Christian Faith,* and a significantly enlarged and revised third edition of his *Soliloquies* came out in 1822. Also among his earlier published works, new or revised material appeared in the following publications: The 1806 *Christmas Eve Celebration* was significantly altered in its second edition (1827), and a newly added volume III.1 (1828) of his already famous Greek-to-German translations of Plato's written works, which are still available from several presses, this time on *"The State,"* books 1–10, with annotations (626 pages). Equally famous works include his lengthy treatise about the doctrine of the Trinity (1822, ET 1835); two versions of his *Christian Ethics* lectures from 1822–23, edited by Jonas in SW I.12 (1843, ET of selections by Brandt 2011); and from 1826–27, critically edited by Hermann Peiter (2011). During the twelve years between 1819 and 1832 he lectured five times, the first to do so critically, on the life of Jesus. The final version of this material was published only in SW I.6 (1864) and in English translation of *The Life of Jesus* by Verheyden and Gilmour (1975). He also wrote prefaces to the second edition of his selected *Predigten* (1820) and to the third edition (1821), and all three sets were collected in one edition, twelve sermons each, in 1830–1831. He kept on publishing sermons, and he continued to offer various arrays of lectures and other written material from 1830 through 1833, much of which also saw early publication, not to be outlined here. Battles over the liturgical agenda and dangers of being dismissed from various regal appointments were continually present throughout his adult years, but, obviously, his efforts did not slacken, and, by and large, they were successful.

Quite rightly, Nowak chooses to treat each strand of Schleiermacher's life during each of the two periods (between 1807 and 1834). What we find, however, differs in that I see much greater continuity of his involvements throughout the life cycle, I note clearer signs of how the several key thematic areas developed over time, and I identify more degrees and descriptions of those areas more broadly as activities to be counted as "works." Thus far, available literature tends to fall short of ideal in this respect, for it is indeed difficult to keep all the interconnected strands and their development in mind (and in one's heart) at the same time.

Finally, to augment Nowak's account of how Schleiermacher experienced his family during the 1820s, we must visit his household, where, to me, Schleiermacher is shown to have been constantly engaged, lovingly and to good effect, with his wife and six children, especially during the 1820s and until his death. This was a huge investment. As problems arose as to his wife and children, and, by their reports, he dealt with those problems tolerably well. In 1820 his family household, mostly in a *Pfarrerhaus* (a manse or parsonage) at Kannonier Strasse 1, at a corner about one block from the university, was coheaded by his wife, Henriette Sophia Elizabeth Schleiermacher (1788–1840). His wife had been born into the noble von Mühlenfels clan, and in 1807 was widowed after Schleiermacher's friend, army chaplain Ehrenfried von Willich (1773–1807) had died. The two were betrothed in 1808, had to wait a year to enter the manse, so were able to marry only in 1809. See Heinrich Meisner's highly noteworthy, hefty edition of Schleiermacher's correspondence with his bride (1923, 1929) and an earlier, two-volume biography edited by him containing correspondence with family and friends (1922).The KGA is still issuing newly supplied volumes of Schleiermacher's vast, continual correspondence, organized by periods in his life and is itself a major work from his pen.

Over the years, other caretakers beside Frau Henriette also served lengthy periods in two Schleiermacher homes—one where they lived most of the year, and the second where they lived during the summer term. Schleiermacher's vacations were taken either alone or with his wife or usually with the children in the break between the summer and winter terms; family vacations happened chiefly for the children's benefit and edification. From 1817 on, they all lived together at Wilhelm Strasse 73. Their primary housing from then on was at the right end of that enormous building, purchased for home and business by his friend, political ally, and publisher Georg Andreas Reimer (1776–1742). (I saw this place years ago; at the right end was a garden where Schleiermacher's children could play and an entrance for the newly added household.) At the first address there was especially his half sister Anna Maria Louise, called Nanny (1786–1869), who had lived with him elsewhere before his new wife arrived in Berlin during 1809. After several years on Wilhelm Strasse, Nanny married Ernst Moritz Arndt (1769–1860), with whom Schleiermacher had been a political comrade since 1807; the newlyweds formed a family in Heidelberg, and they all remained in close contact. His elder sister Friederike Charlotte, called Lotte (1765–1831), was an unwed, permanent member of the Herrnhutter Brethren. When she was not living at the Brethren's sister-house in Berlin, she also joined the Schleiermacher household for extended periods. The longest-staying addition to the Schleiermacher household, Frau Karoline Fischer, was an army officer's widow, a practitioner of hypnotic arts (mesmerism), and an intimate companion of Frau Henriette. Frau Fischer née Lommatsch came to live with the Schleiermachers, with her half-grown daughter Luise in tow. The two mothers, Henriette and Karoline, lived together long after Schleiermacher's death. Unfortunately but predictably, although she might have been controllable, useful, and effective, Frau Fischer, Schleiermacher found, exercised a strong influence on his wife, leading to more stress than records would seem to indicate. There was also a constant traffic of visitors, and once per week he had lunch at home with the assistant pastor then current, who was shared from 1820 on with his then newly appointed Lutheran copastor and academic colleague, Philipp Konrad Marheineke (1780–1846). Although from 1818 to 1831 Georg Wilhelm Friedrich Hegel (1779–1831), a politically conservative idealist philosopher, was a constant thorn in Schleiermacher's side since he himself brought Hegel to Berlin's University. He was not known to accompany Schleiermacher very much anywhere, but he had indeed won over Marheineke. Usually living with poet and publicist Achim von Arnim (1781–1831) in a western territory of Germany, the noted literary figure Bettinna von Arnim, born of the noble Brentano family in that far region, was a household familiar in Schleiermacher's last years and days. He tended to visit his long-term closest female friend, Henriette Herz (1764–1847), called Jette, at her home, especially during her famous evening "sociality" (salon) events.

A latecomer after the five earlier children lived only nine years (1821–1829). This only-begotten son of Schleiermacher, *Nathanael* Hermann, who swiftly died from cholera on October 29, 1829, was the apple of his father's eye—gifted, vigorous, much looked after by his father, and greatly mourned by the entire family. Schleiermacher was deeply struck by this loss.

Nonetheless, he also cared for, appreciated, and encouraged the other six remaining children in the household, and he was sustained, in part, by continuing to be in a fine parenting relationship to them. His wife had brought two of them with her into the marriage. The elder one also bore her mother's name, Henriette von Willich (1805–1886), and thus was fifteen years old in 1820. Her brother bore his deceased father's name, Ehrenfried von Willich (1807–1880).

This son's book describing family life has rarely been cited, but it contains firsthand information from an elder son. Schleiermacher's three daughters came into the world in the following order. Born on Christmas Eve, Clara Elizabeth (1810–1883) arrived the day before Schleiermacher delivered an earlier sermon in the present collection. In 1820 she reached ten years of age. Her later married name was Goldschmidt. Next was Hanna Gertrude (1812–1839), age eight in 1820. The family's final girl was Hildegard Marie (1817–1889), who became the baroness von Schwerin in 1834. Thus, not counting Luise Fischer, the spread of the children's ages in 1820 was from newborn to fifteen, in 1829 from Nathanael's nine years until his death in late October, to Ehrenfried's twenty-five years. Accordingly, Schleiermacher met with a great many higher-pitched voices in that household made up chiefly of women and young children, with only Ehrenfried's changing voice, nearer his own, in the1820s. Surely his intense engagements with all these individuals amount to a considerable work of some sort. At least his language in the 1826–1827 *Christian Ethics* lectures would lead me to think that it would be supremely valued by him in terms of "efficacy" (*Wirksamkeit*), or "efficacious action" (*wirksame Handlung*).

Probably, Nowak's naming the period of the 1820s a *Hohe* (a high point) of Schleiermacher's life refers chiefly to his emerging higher social status. Without a doubt, however, he had already reached that point by 1806, when the king appointed him to a senior pastor position at Charity General Hospital in Berlin (1796–1802). After a two-year pastoral-preaching stint at Stolpe in northeastern Prussia (1802–1804), and his publishing a lengthy, still neglected major book on previous ethical systems (1803), Schleiermacher was appointed by the king to a preaching-professorial post at the University of Halle between 1804 and 1806; this was interrupted by Napoleon's army. In Prussia, the land of

Schleiermacher's birth, such clergy already had high, if not precisely aristocratic, social rank. In 1807, service to his country both as a "patriotic preacher"—as Johannes Bauer (1908) has dubbed him—and as an active creator of principles for a "reform government" conducted by Heinrich Friedrich Karl Freiherr vom und zum Stein (which itself would have enabled, and did partly achieve, greater representative participation under the monarch), and by his taking official coded messages from Berlin to the king, who had moved his household to Königsberg in the northeast to escape Napoleon's grasp in war, Schleiermacher was already significantly established in clerical, academic, and political roles by the close of 1807. These roles he continued to exercise as an acknowledged servant-leader and critic during the rest of his life.

So, what could *Hohe* actually mean? *Hohe* was not a middle-aged "prime of life"; it was not the "zenith" of life or an advantaged position; neither was it high status in that period alone. In short, it makes no sense to use *Hohe* as a descriptor at all. When Schleiermacher preached about persons of "advantage," as in a Christmas sermon, he had to be including himself, at least since he began work as a preacher and as a tutor at the von Dohna estate (1790–1791), from which he carried memories of spending joyful time with children of more ages than even of his own large brood of six or seven children later on in Berlin. Their voices would continue to ring out in his memory as a few of them would leave home before he finally left this same home, deceased at barely sixty-five years of age. These voices would mingle with post horns sighing on the high street not far away, where horse hooves would be clacking, as would wagon and carriage wheels on cobblestoned passages just outside. For him, all the domains in which he pursued tasks of life were organically interconnected and of equal importance ethically, speaking strictly as a devout Christian or more generally as a philosopher and scientific scholar.

9

Various Ways Tidings of the Redeemer Were Received

Second Day of Christmas
Monday, December 26, 1831[1]

When the angels had left them and gone into heaven, the shepherds said to one another: "Let us go now to Bethlehem and see this thing that has taken place, which the Lord has made known to us." So they went with haste and found Mary and Joseph, and the child lying in the manger. When they saw this, they made known what had been told them about this child; and all who heard it were amazed at what the shepherds told them. But Mary treasured all these words and pondered them in her heart. The shepherds returned, glorifying and praising God for all that they had heard and seen, as it had been told them.

—LUKE 2:15–20 (NRSV)

---

1. Among a small number of sermons for which two versions are extant, the slightly corrected version first preached on December 25 under a different title—"The Very First Appearance of the Redeemer as Proclamation of the Joy that Awaits Human Beings"—is omitted here. The biblical text was Luke 2:10–11. The initial publication in a local, limited edition of the sermon preached on Christmas Day (1832), 38–54, is also available in SW II.2 (1835), 132–42; (1843), 137–47. The second version, offered in translation here, was preached on an early Monday morning, the second day of Christmas, December 26, 1831. It appeared among his *Christliede Festpredigten,* vol. II (1833), 100–122, then in SW II.2 (1834, 1843), 329–42, with a different biblical text (Luke 2:15–20) and title.

My devout friends, this further continuation of the gospel narrative of the Redeemer's birth describes for us the impression that the first tidings of it brought forth, and, naturally, the various states of mind and heart that this narrative explicates before us also make a quite varied impression on us. Only too gladly, however, and perhaps also all too easily, do we pass over those who simply wanted to inquire about the facts of the matter, over those who were simply marveling at the story they had heard, and we remain exclusively with the narrative by which, to be sure, what is excellent is spoken, namely, that Mary pondered all these words in her heart. All things considered, however, in general terms, this narrative, as it were, offers us a concise embodiment of various ways people have received tidings concerning the Redeemer, of various impressions this event tended to make on them, and of the part they were taking in it. Indeed, in a certain way we may say that the same relationship we find herein has also continued in just this varied manner almost everywhere and at all times in the world to which the mere proclamation of Christ has come. Yet, if, on the one hand, we should want to be just and fair to those human beings, but, on the other hand, we should also want to understand the divine decree in its full complexity and in its mode of implementation, then in every respect we must not stop with what is immediately evident or simply follow the impression that various ways in which the Redeemer was received has immediately made on us. Rather, we must take into our minds and hearts every detail in its connection to and in its relationship with the rest, just as each aspect takes its place within the whole if we view it all in a proper manner. Therefore, my devout friends, let us first consider these aspects individually. Then let us consider them in their relationship to the current makeup of Christian community.

I

To be sure, it is very common to say that among all those who call themselves Christians there is always but a small portion of whom it may be said, as of Mary, that they ponder these words in their hearts. Indeed, there are some people from whom one must not withhold the attestation that they take part in what is going on just as those shepherds did, and that they are not discouraged from inquiring into the stories told and from thinking about the actual facts of the matter. Yet, ever and again most people would simply be marveling at what is said to them. Much truth lies even in this latter regard, moreover. It would indeed express a wholly improper opinion, however, if we were to proceed based on the presupposition that this gradation of responses would occur to such a degree only in the case of this greatest of events, though it might turn out to be like this everywhere. So that we do not give way too soon to an unfounded cause of complaint, let us first of all see whether we do not observe something similar in all other human events, probably something evident regardless of where we might look.

Let us begin with what for all of us is certainly most trivial and most insignificant, and this is the way that the external aspect of earthly life in its diverse circumstances turns out one way for one human being and differently for another; or let us advance further to what is already far more important for all of us, because it coincides more exactly with this greatest matter of our blessing, or salvation, namely, given development of spiritual powers in someone who exists within our circle. Therein, to be sure, all do participate but each to a rather different degree. Throughout we find this to be the real story, just as it is in this passage. Suppose that something significant and new has appeared in one of the different arenas that are masked out within its telling. However excellent it may be, there always will be very few who immediately grasp the story in its proper sense—that is, as it relates in terms of truth to their specific life circle, and consequently, with joyful confidence, interweaving it enters into their own plans that subsequently they would test anew and in this way advance undisturbed into the proper appreciation of what they preferred to see in the story.[2]

Now, the great multitude always appears to us to be at best similar to those in our text of whom it is said that they heard the story and marveled at what they had heard. So, even in those arenas the greatest part of human beings goes along through life in dull indifference—just as also in the case of our text many were surely like this: in such indefinite, uncertain movements of mind and heart as marveling would be, regardless of any new excitement it might bring more dreaming through life than striding through it with clear consciousness and a firm will.

---

2. Characteristics of these observers describe major aspects of how Schleiermacher himself had long proceeded with much of what he saw or had been told. Together, these aspects include strong elements of contemplation, observation of interconnected factors, and reflection, combined with an amending process of inquiry, investigation and evaluation that lead to actual consequences and that define a pragmatic set of habits. See just below for more on what they would do.

Fewer in number but, to be sure, by far more significant are those who are stirred to reflection and to inquiring into everything new that happens in human life, just as it is said of the shepherds here, that they wanted to go and see how matters stood with the story, which they had heard from the angels. Moreover, as it is said of the shepherds after they had found the facts of the matter agreeing with the description, they returned and praised and glorified God. So it occurs also in the case of many who might have been inquiring. If after careful investigation something new seems to them so significant and beneficial than what was commended to them at first, they thankfully turn their gaze upward and happily await further unfolding. Indeed, like the shepherds of our text, infrequently they also add that they have called the attention of others to the event and have borne witness to it as they have found it. There is always only the fewest number of those persons who are also soon permeated so inwardly in their minds and hearts by whatever has come to be known to them as new and good that it merges into their very lives. As a result, they also put the story in touch with everything that they would otherwise ponder. In every respect, they likewise take it into consideration, and their doing so helps to define them. In short, it immediately begins to get firm and to take hold within them.

Thus, my good friends, when we see that such a variety of responses runs through all human circumstances, indeed that even in the external relations of a person to the goods and forces of this earth, most people by far do not attain to full possession of what seems to be within everyone's provenance. Even less do human beings come to proper consciousness about how we should exist in this relation to earth's goods and forces.

We may wonder that the same gradations occur even in this spiritual arena, on the question of human beings' consciousness of their relationship to God! There should be no complaint about this. Rather, we must convince ourselves that all these matters express the decree[3] of God, and that it all belongs essentially to the level at which the human spirit stands in this life. What is best and most excellent requires a large foundation where we are. In any given instance, a great many have to be present so that only a few can rise to a certain height over the others in a certain order from that point on, so as, in turn, to discharge over the whole the richness of goods that had fallen to them as their share.

3. The reference is to "the one eternal divine decree." See "decree" in the Analytical Index of *Christian Faith* (2016).

Now, however, after we have considered this process in general terms, as the divine decree and as our human destiny on earth, let us go on to contemplate more closely precisely this variety of responsiveness, especially in reference to the new tidings concerning the Redeemer's birth as its happening is presented in our story about his birth. Those who seem to obtain least benefit from sheer proclamation about the Redeemer are undeniably among those who hear and marvel at the shepherds' agreement with the angels' news: It is said that they both heard the angels' message and marveled at it. However, my good friends, suppose that we consider this part of the story more closely. Then, we will have to say not only that we would act very wrongly if we wanted to judge and condemn these individuals because they had not also done the same thing as did the others, namely, going about to look for the child and to spread the report about him even more broadly. Let us rather first admit that the shepherds are not the worst by far. Would it not have been natural enough if among themselves all had thought: This event is only one more of those very same follies that have appeared in our time, arousing empty hopes? Before the times of Christ and afterwards, among the people there were indeed a great many who did not interpret the prophecies of the Old Testament with proper understanding! Just so, could not many have thought: What sort of child has been born today does not concern us? Moreover, they might have thought, no matter whether the child might turn out to be the one about whom the prophecies of the Old Testament have spoken, nevertheless before the child were to grow up and become a man, before the child could step up and show how he is destined to be king in the name of Supreme Being, and in what sense he were to become a savior of the people, we wouldn't be around to see this. So, why should we care any further about something with which we actually have nothing to do, something that can addend only to the good of our descendants? Now, those who would have thought this way would also not even have marveled at the event! To marvel is thus always the mind's and heart's already being inclined toward a given subject. At the very least, to marvel would attest to an open sensibility, and indeed without any selfish reference to oneself, to a sensibility open to everything that, in general terms, is important for a human being, and this, to be sure, would already be a commendable elevation above a customary response.

Hence, before we condemn these people, let us ask: What would the Redeemer have said about them? Moreover, this will not be difficult for us to discover if we reflect on something that he once uttered when one of his disciples wanted to punish a stranger who had driven out spirits in the name of Jesus but did not actually follow him. On occasion he would say: "One cannot easily perform an act in my name and subsequently speak evil of me; who is not against us is for us."[4] We could well apply these words also to such individuals as these if we were to say that one who has been so moved by such a story that one pays attention to it, that one marvels in face of it, if given one's marveling once it has become pronounced, one cannot soon thereafter slander the subject of one's interest. This would be so, for therewith this individual would have to be slandering his or her own excitement, just as if one wanted to slander the person whose name one had used to accomplish something fine and important. Indeed, all those who do not also go further, as the Gospels and the original proclamation of Christ have done, simply in that precisely this entire divine arrangement, the way it has happened therewith, the further continuation of the event, and the shape of matters human by means of the event would all be subjects for them to marvel at. These individuals would indeed always be bearers of the divine Word, and thus, even if only in an indirect way, they would be instruments of the divine Spirit. The Word would be set in motion by them, for no one would have been silent while at the same time marveling at something. Often the event might turn again into one's sensibility, and if the event were a matter of attaching something significant to one's sensibility, that process might itself, in turn, also be immediately facing one's very soul. Accordingly, for each individual this marveling is a stage of preparation both for the connection of a closer relationship with the Redeemer and for having a more or less significant effect on the whole inasmuch as one would be standing within the whole that one is oneself facing.

Now, let us move on to take a good look at the shepherds, of whom it is first said that they spoke among themselves: Let us go to Bethlehem, they said, and witness the story that has been told to us. Let us see whether it is really like what we have been told. Furthermore, let us then observe how they subsequently spread the story and glorified and praised God for all that they had heard and seen. At this point, to be sure, we cannot deny that they would have advanced farther than did the other individual whom we discussed. Yet, more than what they accomplished was also not to be required under the given circumstances. To be sure, my good friends, when we consider ourselves and our relationship to the

4. Mark 9:38–40 (NRSV).

Redeemer, in its entire compass this event might appear to be something quite small. It was indeed something commendable that those shepherds did not immediately ignore the word of the angels, whereby they, as it were, would have snuffed it out. Rather, after they themselves had received a sign that they could look into, they wanted to inquire whether matters stood in accordance with the sign. Moreover, after they had found it to be so, they immediately also directed the attention of others to this story and came to the aid of the angels' message, in that they first narrated it to those who were in the immediate surroundings of the child but then also brought word about the event to others. Moreover, one notices that they, as it were, did not consider the matter to be one of indifference. Rather, they were affected by it within their minds and hearts and truly expected something great from it all and for their entire people. One grasps this based on the fact that it is said of them that they had praised and glorified God. However, to be sure, no narrative in our Gospels offers any further mention of them, whether one or another of them was subsequently among the Lord's disciples, or whether in general and at the time when the Redeemer appeared in public someone among the shepherds was still present who could call attention to the fact that Jesus was the same person about whom it had been spoken in such and such a way upon his arrival in the world. Apparently, this lack of any further report might cast a detrimental light on them, but how soon was the Redeemer not moved out of their sight, how little were they in a position from then on to follow his further leadership in the world! Moreover, even if one or another of the shepherds was still living when the Redeemer appeared in public, how little cause would they have even simply to suppose that he was the same person about whom it had been spoken to them at that earlier event? This could be so, especially in that he came from a totally different area, from Galilee, and it was generally believed that he was also born there. Furthermore, he was not appearing as they would have been inclined to expect according to that proclamation. Rather, he appeared simply as a teacher, of which there were many among the folk! Thus, we must admit that it would be an unfair expectation to demand more of them than they themselves did, and we would have no right to find fault with them on that account or to value their glorifying and praising God less because afterwards they would not have entered into any closer connection with the Redeemer.

Ah, my good friends, suppose that we were properly to imagine the destiny of such individuals in that era. We would indeed have to admit that the angel of the Lord's being directed with its proclamation precisely to these shepherds, shows itself to be a very wise choice. In the same situation, how many others would have remained completely indifferent and would have said among themselves: "Even if a king may be born for future generations, nothing good will come to us from that! So, now as ever, as shepherds we would spend our lives with our flocks, our destiny would not come to be anything but what it has been up to now." Moreover, if the shepherds of old had borne in this same cold attitude toward everything that did not affect them, avoiding the joyful proclamation they had heard, word of the event would have passed by them in vain!

How must we not already highly respect it when, placed in a position such as these shepherds had, someone would have raised oneself above what is immediately nearest, would have taken part in more nearly general concerns, and would also have rejoiced in what generally is to come to the good of human beings, even if not in any way to this one actual individual! This raising of oneself above the present and above what would directly affect oneself is already a beautiful and noble level at which one particular human soul would stand. In such a soul, the divine Word would already have had an overall effect—one that would be lacking in many others. This would be so, for a tendency to inculcate what is divine is also to be assumed where such a rising above what is immediately present and sensory is perceived. Moreover, it was nevertheless not possible for them to pursue this story further in its unfolding—a story about which they inquired with such interest and spoke of with such feeling, also a story that inspired them to such praise of God! Can we blame them for not pursuing the story further? Must we not say that the way their lives and the Redeemer's life were led depended on the divine order, according to which a closer, more direct connection with him in consequence of this proclamation that we have examined was not granted to them?

II

Now, from this point on, let us consider these various points of view in their interconnectedness with the way that the Christian community as a whole is now formed among us. To be sure, within it many share the name of Christian with us, but they would actually seem to belong only among those who simply marvel at this entire phenomenon. Accordingly, we would notice how such a complete transformation of human affairs could have proceeded, even if only gradually, from such an insignificant point. This too would be an object of marvel for the shepherds. We would then notice how the Christian community could have proceeded from a people who had been an object of disregard for other peoples for a long time already, a people who by their law would seem to have excluded themselves from having a direct influence on other peoples and, for that reason, were at times more despised, at times more hated by other peoples. We may then ask: How could an individual belonging to this particular people have become such a subject of widespread acclaim and devotion for so many other peoples? How could faith in an eminent, close relationship between God and the Redeemer arise among them, and how could this teaching be propagated so widely among hugely diverse groups of human beings? Yet, most of all, how could this faith still exist even now? How could it exist, regardless of how sufficiently clear and evident it might be that, in part, among those who profess the name of this Redeemer the same weaknesses and imperfections are customary, and the faithful are therefore also affected by the same afflictions and restrictions of life as other humans are—also, in part, whether no actual traces of a higher life are to be found among most of them?

This situation, as we noticed, is, for many who likewise call themselves Christians even today, simply an object of marvel. To be sure, this disparity would be small if people should really want to be Christians, and yet I would gladly like to convince you that even this marveling has already grasped hold of something very true within the matter itself. Obviously, underlying all of these considerations is the supposition that if matters were like this with Christ, as we believe, and if such a difference between him and all other human beings truly existed, then something much greater within humankind would also have to have been caused by this Christian community of faith if the relationship of Christians to Christ were simply to have possessed the proper power and ardency. Apparently, this proper state of feeling is fundamental to the very marveling that we are addressing today. Must we not admit, moreover, that this process of marveling is already a highly effective preparation,[5] and that such persons are simply missing the highest illumination of the divine Spirit in order no longer simply to say that if matters stood as is believed, then things would surely be different in the world, but to say this: Yes, matters

5. In *Christian Faith* (2016) under "grace, preparatory" in the Analytical Index.

are still such that the world is not better, and this is simply a sign of how little and how slowly human beings attain to their finding and fulfilling their true destiny on earth! Thus, this would also be a sign of how immeasurable the distance is, in fact, between the one who put up this flag of blessedness, or salvation, and those who, as it were, involuntarily follow that flag but yet do not themselves take a definite part in the glory and praise of the Redeemer in the splendor of their inner life, which was in him and is to proceed from him! Accordingly, must we not say that such a marveling already bears within itself a stirring that can lead a human being to true blessedness, or salvation? Indeed, must we not also say that it takes a very little stirring of this sort for one to be still far removed from a true, full enjoyment of God's reign?[6]

So, let us now go further and look at those members of the Christian community who, just like those shepherds, present themselves to us as persons who diligently seek out the stories to which the faith of Christians refers, and who also make everything that is told to us about them, viewed as coming down from above, the subject of their reflection. Indeed, it necessarily belongs to this task that they definitely distinguish this occurrence of the Redeemer's birth from all other equally important events when they diligently seek out this occurrence before all others, wondering how credible everything that has been handed down to us is and wondering as to whether something false has perhaps gotten mixed in with what is true. If these members of the Christian community should find the purported facts of the matter to be such that their historical foundation remains firm, then this finding might help us spread the account given in the story, each presenting the stories of Jesus in one's own manner, viewing them as highly important and significant beyond comparison with others' stories. Each would then be praising and glorifying God for this event, in that they would trace everything they see to be unfolding in the world among Christian peoples back to the one person in whom it has its origin. In the Evangelical Church we have had a great many persons pursuing this task from its very beginning onwards. Yet, how are they usually appraised? As we have also judged the shepherds earlier, it is said that among those storytellers, people miss this inner movement of the heart, as compared with Mary, who is said to have pondered all these words in her heart. To be sure, the Word was not spoken without effect to all who took part in the story. Those who received the

6. In the Christian domain "God's reign" (a preferred substitute for "kingdom of God" equates with "the invisible church." See *Christian Faith* (2016), §§150–52.

story would also have gotten moving on behalf of the Word, searching into the story and letting others partake of it, and also praising God for it! However, regarding them one might not notice enough in order to see that another life has arisen within them, a life based on the story, or, in other words, to see that they have entered into the most intimate, most personal relationship with the Redeemer. In a certain way, this accusation may likely be true of a great many persons who occupy a significant role among inquiring, reflective minds and hearts in the telling of this story. However, if they have made especially this story the subject of their inquiry, viewed as an especially important one, if they could not have imagined anything important in it besides its interconnectedness with God's decree, would they then not have to have become aware of and, in their own fashion, gain surety about the fact that this storied birth of Jesus also especially comes from God? Whatever the case might be, moreover, we may ask: In how many ways are such persons not instruments of the divine Spirit! In particular, how important has the service of such persons not been for the work of improvement within the Christian church itself! How much have they not contributed to our return from being human institutions by which the church's life was distorted to the purity of the Gospels! How much such candid and true inquiry about the actual facts of Christianity's history in general would not have contributed to this restoration of Christian truth,[7] so that a simple Evangelical faith could never have reached a proper surety without taking this renewed spiritual direction! Who can overlook any of these features today?

Now, if such activity has been so helpful to human beings again, their having been able properly to enjoy God's blessedness, or salvation, and if those who are engaged in these inquiries are such important instruments that God avails Godself to them for support of divine truth, could we then possibly believe that in their own inner life nothing of this process would addend to their good? Certainly, just as an individual can be an instrument of the divine Spirit, this more or less directly, so too there can be a less or a more direct consciousness and consequently a varied enjoyment of divine grace. Must not everything that is the glorification and praise of God come from God? Must not everything that is the glorification and praise of God because of Christ be traced back to Christ? Suppose, moreover, that many would thus also acknowledge and honor the Redeemer of the world, especially given his role in history

---

7. See *Christian Faith* (2016), Analytical Index, pertinent items under "truth," "Christianity," and "church."

as it has developed through him, especially in the pure thought belonging to the higher destination of his life as a human being in this world, especially in the pure spiritual love that he fostered toward us and that flowed through him into us, especially in his striving for a higher peace and for the blessed enjoyment of God's presence! Then, if many do particularly acknowledge and honor him for these reasons alone, should we not gladly admit that they are attached to him, even if not in just as direct and personal a relationship of love and attachment as we and many others are? Accordingly, the diversity that exists among the followers of Christ does indeed seem to us to be less than we might have imagined originally, and we must be pleased in the face of this diversity!

In our final reflection, let us devote a few words to looking at Mary as well—Mary, about whom it is said that she kept all these words in mind and pondered them in her heart. Let us also consider those who most correspond to her in Christian community. Yes, Mary was, to be sure, especially favored among women![8] There were more virgins than she in Israel, and even more virgins from the tribe of David—if it was indeed necessary that the Savior had to be born from this tribe. However, she was the one chosen by God. That she pondered the words in her heart, ah, that was very natural and easy to explain, because it so closely concerned her personally, because yet another such angelic message was added to what she herself had already experienced in similar fashion. Further, my good friends, suppose that we now ask ourselves: Was the fact that she pondered the words in her heart already the proper beatific faith, was it already completely the fruitful seed of such a personal relationship to the Redeemer as we might have imagined it to be when we have received that faith, viewed as something exalted or supreme? At that moment Mary was already firm and unshakeable in the belief that she had been considered worthy, and in such a way that the Savior of the world was to see the light of this earth through her? Our books of the Bible all too clearly enable us to understand the very opposite. Long afterward, when the Redeemer was already teaching, there was a time when she wavered between him and his brothers, who did not believe him to be the Redeemer, when she went to him with those brothers in the intention of taking him out of his career, thinking him to be mad, in order to draw him back into her narrower domestic circle.[9] Thus, despite

8. See the index to find earlier discussions regarding Jesus' mother and Schleiermacher's own mother.

9. Mark 3:21, 32.

her earlier so much deeper, more internal pondering in her soul about the words that had been spoken about the child, this child would have seen the light of the world through her. At this time, Mary's personal bliss was in no way firmly grounded.

Accordingly, my good friends, we will probably always have to say that this is how it is with all persons who are considered worthy of such a closer, inner personal association with the Redeemer. With others too, steadfastness of heart is simply a work that takes time. With others too, the process of getting firmly grounded passes through several instances of temptation and vacillation. Moreover, what we already said before is valid for all the others, as it was for Mary. It is a special blessing that they are placed in a closer relationship to the Redeemer in life, that they are ever more awakened anew by everything that affects them, and that they are always driven to ponder anew the words that are registered in their hearts. The seed of one's lacking in faith is also within them, however, and within them too it is overcome only little by little, with the result that gradually faith comes to be so strong in them that all of life appears as a worthy testimony of this faith that has gained strength.

Still further, my good friends, what is now the conclusion to which we are coming, given our reflections? It is this: The Redeemer is given to the world. That is, he is given to humankind—and, quite surely, the blessedness, or salvation, of humankind will always proceed only from him and will be advanced by him. However, it would be a precarious matter if we should want to measure the part a given individual has therein, and in this way, comparing that one human being with some other, want to express a firm judgment that would all too easily be a hard one, on the one hand, and a partial one, on the other hand. An individual human being is never and nowhere alone. It is a matter of divine grace when anyone is called sooner and closer to the Redeemer. However, we must also consider everything that simply directs one's attention to that eternal inheritance which he brings and which simply raises one human being above earthly life and in some way holds one fast within the vast circle in which the Word of the Redeemer is both efficacious and life-giving. We must consider it all to be a matter of divine grace, to be a genuine advantage and blessing that simply befalls a human being. Likewise, however, no one, on the other hand, should consider one's part in the Redeemer's blessings to be a possession as well, something that one could have for oneself alone! Just as everything of this kind is a work of divine grace,[10] so we too have everything not for ourselves alone, but for everyone. If we now celebrate the Redeemer's coming on earth, if we ponder these words in our hearts, let us never remain alone with ourselves in such actions. Rather, let us consider that he is the blessing, or salvation, of the world, and that we also have to let everything that effects this blessing, or salvation, in our minds and hearts be effective in others' lives as well.

Accordingly, may the proper marveling at this impenetrable guidance of humankind then never cease to be operative in the Christian church, for thereby the attention of others is also aroused! May searching into these stories, which are indeed the greatest ones that ever occurred within the whole of humankind, never end, for thereby truth is always placed in brighter light! Let us never stop talking about these stories and spreading the Word concerning them in order that it may remain vital wherever we are and have some effect. Let us never cease to glorify and praise God also for that which is said to each of us especially. That is to say, it is given for our benefit, for our own experience and also for receiving information that we can have about the matter at hand. However, then, to be sure, let us also ever continue to ponder the words from God that reside in our hearts. So that we may reach the proper goal, especially for ourselves as Christians, let us assiduously inquire as to how these words come to be efficacious, and inquire as to what use we are to make of them. Let us ask how we may come to know how to value the fact that we are born and raised in the Lord's community, and that therefore his name is so often in our hearing and must naturally so often be in our mouths as well, so that his image cannot disappear from our sight. Let us ask whether we too are ennobled and sanctified ever more by all of this. However, let us deem all blessings that are granted to ourselves as a common good, just as the apostle Paul says that all gifts are to prove themselves to be effective as a benefit held in common. However, in order that we, on the other hand, may also properly consider the common state of things, let us not look upon each individual person as to whether this person already has gained what is of supreme value. Rather, on the one hand, let us delight in the unmistakable effects of the Gospels on the whole, and, on the other hand, let us make joyous use of our own share of divine blessings as far as each of us can reach within one's own circle. That is to say, this is the sole correct path of joyful faith by which we are able to

---

10. See *Christian Faith* (2016), Analytic Index under "grace."

do our share to spread the Word and to increase the praise and glory of the one of whom we know and profess that, in fact, blessing, or salvation, is in his name alone. Before him all knees must bow among those who live on earth, so that we all may recognize in him the glory of the only begotten Son of the Father. Amen.

Editor's Postscript

Just as, over eight years, early sermons had expanded themes from the first edition of Schleiermacher's *Christian Faith* (1821–1822), so this 1831 sermon expands on themes from the second edition of *Christian Faith* (1830–1831). The sermon also adds detail and structure to Schleiermacher's Christmas sermons; it imagines experiences of the first participants on the first evening of Jesus' birth. The final two sermons, given in 1832 and 1833, add further meaning to this event, which foretells the significance of Jesus' entire work of redemption in the full life of the Redeemer, "the Son of God," through his birth, through his upbringing through young adulthood, and then through his mature ministry to the point of death, into eternal life. To him, all this development occurred by the grace and Spirit of God, eventually through the free, invisibly determined influence of the Christian church. All his sermons, whether for festive occasions or for other points in the church year, are to be interpreted in the light of the multiply explicated, constantly developing themes of these Christmas sermons. Like all his sermons, these Christmas sermons are based on constant exegetical examination of New Testament texts. Readers must recognize that as taken down and translated into English, all Schleiermacher's sermons bear at least slight limitations: They are subject to checking with theological texts formed solely by him, and they are subject to scrutiny and comparison with other scriptural texts and in rare cases with shortcuts available in the Christian tradition. Thus, as Schleiermacher frequently declared, all reflection and observances within the Christian church are bound to develop to the end of days, perhaps beyond that eschaton, as long as humanity exists. Schleiermacher never intended to form either law or school. Instead, his aim was to foster the internal purification, the proper external growth, the structural reform, and the worldwide communal life of the church. Given this aim, the 1820 sermon, which I recently published and explicated elsewhere encapsulates how his earlier Christian sermons prepared for the systematically structured presentation of the first edition of *Christian Faith* (1821–1822), just as the Christmas sermons especially from 1823 through 1831 explored themes also to be contained in the 1830–1831 *Christian Faith* revised second edition and those from 1832 and 1833 and further might have continued to extend that account for many years to come had he not reached death on February 14, 1834 as this one does, albeit rather in a narrow and refined compass.

10

The Appearance of the Redeemer as the Basis for the Restitution of True Equality among Humankind

Second Day of Christmas, December 26, 1832[1]

Glory to God in the Highest and Peace on Earth
among People in Whom God is Well-Pleased.

As many of you as were baptized into Christ have clothed yourselves
with Christ. There is no longer Jew or Greek, there is no longer slave or
free, there is no longer male and female; for all of you are one in Christ
Jesus.
—GAL 3:27–28 (NRSV)

My devout listeners, what we have now heard here in one another's company reminds us of the manifold inequality that occurs among people, an
inequality about which we do indeed have to say that it coincides with sin
just as much as death does. Inequality is the work and the wages of sin,
all the more so as almost everywhere sin becomes the death of that peace

---

1. Ed note: This version, preached on the second day of Christmas, December 26,
1832, was revised for *Christliche Festpredigten*, vol. II (1833), 125–46, also in SW II.2
(1834, 1843), 343–66. The initial version is available for comparison in a local, limited
edition that also appeared in 1833, 171–89.

which coheres so exactly with glorification of God, and sin becomes the death of that love by which God's blessing is best manifested. The more people abandon themselves to those kinds of corruption that mostly have influence on shared life, namely, to a corruptive influence that may arise from selfishness, domineering, vanity, and to other such influence as may arise with all the greater diversity by which inequality also branches out. Moreover, all the more oppressively does inequality then press upon everyone, almost without exception. It does this no less on those who are somehow elevated than on those who are held down. Furthermore, where kindly human imagination dreams of a better condition for things on earth but, at the same time, perceives a high degree of this inequality there, it immediately directs its glance also at inequality, viewed as an evil that first has to be removed before an improved replacement can enter. Still further, every design for an improvement of matters human also takes form as an essential component, here in one way, there in another way. Thereby, a change of those unequal relationships may occur in order to bring them closer to brotherly/sisterly equality, which so well becomes those to whom God has given the earth to rule.[2]

Now, the words of our text also speak of an abolition of this inequality by singling out those formations of it that would have appeared to be the most momentous to the apostle's readers. In this regard, no Jew (if belonging to the people earlier chosen by God) would be in a better position than any other Jew, and no Greek (having come along with the pernicious delusions of superstition and idolatry) would stand in a much lower position than any Jew. In this regard, no one would actually be a free person who is accustomed to ruling over others, and no one would actually be a slave and for that reason looked down upon and thought little of, viewed as a living instrument simply for achieving the will of others. In this regard, surely no one would have been a male human being who would have ruled at that time with unlimited arbitrariness even over the companion of his life; and in this regard, no one would have been a woman who would have been subjected to the arbitrariness of a man and therefore thought to be in a position lower than he—but precisely not so under God's reign.[3]

2. Yes, Schleiermacher does say this, and the notion is biblical, but what does he mean, given that we humans have made such a mess of such a charge, especially if it were taken to have come from God? We shall see!

3. Beginning with this contrast between the actual difference in social status between human females and males is consistent with Schleiermacher's ethical writing

"In Christ Jesus you are all one." Further, my devout friends, the apostle's statement referred not to anything singular or particular that the Redeemer had done, but simply to what he was, to our faith in him as the Son of God who took on flesh, and to the fact that we call upon him and give up our lives into his life. Yet, how this is brought about in the Lord's community in such a manner is also, to be sure, distinct enough from what so many well-disposed people even in our age miss so painfully and wish for so longingly. Hence, we will probably not doubt—if we look at the importance of the matter and simultaneously at how what, as the apostle maintains, coheres with the specific being of the Redeemer, with our fundamental relationship to him—namely, that we would also fill such a festive hour, as our hours of Christmas are, in a worthy and appropriate manner when we consider with one another how the Redeemer's appearance in the world is the proper basis for the restitution, or restoration, of true equality among human beings.

Let us first answer the question as to how and by what means the Redeemer is the basis for such a restitution, and then, second, how and in what manner the proper equality among human beings is also represented in his appearance. May it be this process through which the Lord wants to grant us his blessing in this hour of reflection!

I

If we, my devout listeners, first ask how and by what means the Redeemer's appearance is such a basis for restitution of equality among human beings, and thereby precisely how this manifold, complex inequality would be present in our minds, we will easily agree that we generally trace back inequality in a twofold manner. That is, when we disregard what has its direct basis in the design of human nature and is more a difference, rather than actually an inequality, that has created an advantage of one person over another. Take youth and age, for example: What is that but a difference of place that diverse persons occupy at the same time in our different periods of life? Yet, where the one person is now, the other was there previously, and the former person comes along to the place where the

on inequality since at least his stays in Schlobitten and Landsberg as a young adult (1790–1796) aged twenty-one to twenty-eight. Thus far, the literature on this subject shows him to be a source and support for feminist causes. So, what implications regarding other exploitations against other human rights might flow from his beginning with this one? Again, we shall see!

latter was earlier. Consider the variety in which the human being is differently represented in different regions of the earth in terms of body and soul. What is this if not simply, without evincing any essential inequality, a change in how the human spirit, how human life, is revealed in such and such a living place allotted to it at a particular time of life? Man and woman, what is this but two forms ordered by God for the continuance of human existence on earth—the one just as indispensable and essential as the other, and each one equipped with one's own powers pleasing to God?

However, we trace everything else back, on the one hand, to advantages inherent in a person by birth, and, on the other hand, to advantages that a person acquires during life, in whatever manner it may be, whether more by one's own activity or more by the work of others. Yet, if we want to consider the two exactly, how little are we able to distinguish the one from the other! Consider how we disagree and cannot come to a firm decision about which advantages in one person's life are truly that person's own, already enclosed as seeds in the person's early existence and first brought into the person's life through rearing and education of the child and through interaction with other people. Nevertheless, whether we are able to distinguish each person as an individual (with advantages or not), or whether we see persons as combining with one another in a clear and definite manner or in a manner hidden to us, nevertheless we trace everything back to these two possibilities—either standing primarily as an individual person or existing primarily within a community of persons.

Well then! Suppose, moreover, that we now ask ourselves how and by what means the Redeemer is the basis for cessation of this inequality? What can we give as an answer other than simply to say that by his birth Jesus held an advantage over all other human beings, an advantage against which all other advantages of this kind disappear and can no longer be taken into consideration. Accordingly, compared with the Redeemer's advantage, advantages by birth are all equal. Further, the Redeemer had an advantage in the development of his entire human life up to the consummation, or perfection, of his adult life—an advantage that is found nowhere other than with him. Accordingly, also on this account, under him all other advantages are equal. How could it be possible, my devout friends, for us to celebrate the festival of the Redeemer's birth, how could we truly take into ourselves his appearance, anew within our minds and hearts, without being imbued with results derived from this perfection!

Indeed, it is our shared faith that the Redeemer is born as the one who was given to humankind by God for blessing, or salvation, namely, as the only one of his kind, that he was born as the only begotten Son of God, as the Word become flesh, as the one in whom the fullness of divinity dwelt as long as he was to live and walk upon this earth. However, someone could say, did he not belong especially to a chosen people and singled out among them? Someone may ask, was this not the divinely chosen people precisely because the Redeemer of the world was to be born from among this people, and thereby from that people had not a new inequality just then started to emerge? This would be the case, for precisely because he belonged especially to this people, did not everyone who was of his tribe and was so much more closely related to him in terms of their very human nature, also stand just so much closer to him, the divinely favored one, and consequently did they not have a great advantage over all the others? The Redeemer himself indeed seems to admit and to confirm this point, in that he not only said but also subsequently acted and lived accordingly. He did so in that he himself was sent only to the lost sheep of the house of Israel! Yet, I would reply: How would he himself see this matter? He saw it simply as a necessary limitation of his personal efficacy on earth, an efficacy itself founded in the divine will, thus as a limitation that had its natural basis precisely in the fact that his relationships were to be purely human, and his entire life was to be subject to all the laws of human existence. He saw it simply as a limitation such that for his person he was also to remain among this people, for when he departed from earth he gave his disciples the instruction that now they should no longer stay within this limited situation but should spread out and go out among all peoples and make them disciples and teach them to do what he had taught and commanded. To be sure, only those persons from among the people of the Old Testament who were capable of being elevated to precisely this view could come to have faith in the Redeemer and, at the same time, would always have had to come to a point of clarity about the fact that to belong to the people of the Old Testament was not at all an advantage that afforded them a particular value in and of themselves, but that nevertheless they were held together simply under the same sin to which all human beings had succumbed, to the end that and because the Son of God was to be born from and among them.

However, something else might still seem to us to remain left over, viewed as an essential inequality that first came about through the Redeemer himself. Suppose that amid an identified group of human beings the Word of Life had already been inherent for a long time. Suppose that the soothing divine Spirit had already proven to be efficacious among a people from one generation to another. Suppose too that the fine arrangements of the spiritual temple of God had purified and ennobled human life there and in a manifold manner. Would not those who entered immediately into such a union described then take pleasure in a true advantage by their birth, especially if they had caught sight of the light of the world? Already before their entrance into the world, would a blessing not have been afforded these persons, a blessing from which all of their kind would earlier have been far removed? Here we do not have to speak either of those persons whose lives the Word of God had not penetrated at all, or of those who had just taken in the divine splendor of the Word, those to whom the glad tones of the messengers bringing peace would just recently have come.

To be sure, the matter might well seem like this to us, my devout friends, but who among us will also not claim to recall that when so many kinds of defects do confront us within and throughout the earthly church of the Redeemer, with proper fervor we bear a certain longing for those earlier times of first love! Consider how often we do not then turn, with just as much shame as with reverential admiration, toward those beginnings of the gospel in which such an eagerness would have been shown to us. This would be the same eagerness which we seek in vain among ourselves, a force of the divine Word such as to make humankind free! This force also easily loosens the mostly seductive bonds by which people could be prevented from hearing the words of peace, from embracing the life that comes from God, nevertheless! How the power of the gospel does seem to us so much greater at that time, so much purer, so much stronger, as if in these later times it would have been weakened by its aging.

Yet, the one view is just as one-sided as the other. As the Lord's word is eternal, so too is his mode of efficacious action eternal. Moreover, in itself alone time can neither elevate nor lower this action. Yes, if divine life could be innate in a person, then there might be something in the first view; and, in turn, if divine life could grow obsolete and decline, just as the earthly appearance of a human being passes away from weakness at the end, then something true could attach to the other view. However, the one is no more true than the other. That is to say, all life that springs from the fullness of the Redeemer is everlastingly fresh and young. Its expressions can be eased by practice and also, in turn, rendered difficult, if earthly instruments used lose their versatility. However, what in this manner might seem to us to be old, on the one hand, or seriously lacking and crude, on the other hand, this is not his bearing but is ours alone. Inequality is and remains something that is in us; it is not in him. Rather, this very inequality too is to disappear in and through him. Indeed, inasmuch as we truly exist in him, inequality has also certainly disappeared.

Now, if these inequalities are conditioned by birth, even though they might well stand in the closest respect to our higher, spiritual life, nonetheless they are to be thought of as a nil state if we compare them with the Redeemer's advantage by birth over all human beings, no matter how much all the other advantages might indeed well disappear, the influence of which would extend only to what is external!

Further, what are we to say about the exclusive perfection that is represented for us in the appearance of the Redeemer? If we compare this perfection, or consummation, with such a great difference as that between the wisest human beings and the most foolish ones, between mostly refined persons and the most wrongheaded ones, how, in contrast, does his distance from all of us actually appear? Let us simply follow his perfection from the first beginnings of his life onward up to his public activity and to the accomplishment of his earthly calling. I say from the first beginnings of his life onward, for even if no particular features of these beginnings would have been passed down to us, oh how easily and gladly would faith supplement this lack by adhering to the words indicating that the child advanced in wisdom and grace in his communion with God and with human beings! Into what a lovely image of his childlike purity and innocence, also an image of a joyous development of his spiritual and living strength, do we shape for ourselves the adolescence of the Redeemer, when he would have attained not either but both of these characteristics such that, by virtue of purer surroundings, he would have remained protected against everything that was troublesome and tempting from one level to the next. Rather, already from within he would have had to reject anything that, even if only externally, could bring a whiff of sin to the surface of his life. Moreover, if we were to look first at his more mature age, what perfection could we compare with his own, which he would have expressed most simply when he said: "I and the Father are one"; or, what is one and the same thing, when he said of himself: "The Son can do nothing on his own, but the works that the Father shows him, these he does, and the Father will show him ever greater works"?[4]

4. John 10:30; John 5:19–20.

Thus, his entire life, from the first development on up to his full power and maturity, would have been nothing but an ever farther, ever brighter looking around himself and working, from one moment to the next, in connection with the mysterious, everlasting work of God, which work he had come to accomplish! Given this purity and truth, given this vitality of discernment that would immediately have merged into deed, what claims are to be compared with such as these? When this figure is present in our minds, how it would have borne within itself the foundation and power of such a life from the first beginning of its appearance onward! Then the otherwise apparently great inequality of human beings with a view to development and cultivation of spiritual powers might well have disappeared, as if insignificant! In comparison with this inability to assimilate error, how well indeed might human wisdom itself have appeared, which would then so easily and so enthusiastically consider its notions about nature and the interconnectedness of things to be truth, though generally each next generation, in turn, might well already revoke them! Certainly, as the apostle says: "Here there is no Jew, no Greek, no free person, no slave, no man and no woman." He could also just as well have said: "Here there is no wise person and no simple-minded person; rather, in Christ Jesus you are also all one in this respect." Or does human wisdom ever seem greater to us than when it professes that something more perfect could not be imagined than this pure mind and heart, which offers itself to God for the sins of the entire world; or than this sanctifying love, which embraces the entire human race, in order to suffuse and satiate it with everlasting truth; or than the founding of this universal covenant of faith and of brotherhood and sisterhood, which could be pointed only to him!

Now, suppose that we cannot answer the question as to what is then the proper measure of equality for the Lord's disciples, inasmuch as even they would still have been unequal to him, other than in the following way: Each disciple would have been in the truth as much, and, with one's spiritual power intact, each disciple would have had an effect within one's earthly life as much as each would have let the life of the Redeemer have an effect within oneself and as each would, at the same time, have been recognized by other persons as a true disciple of the one whom God had sent for the blessing, or salvation, of the world. Then, precisely with this thought, it is already said: That here too the Redeemer provides the basis for equality. This would be so, for inequality simply lies within us. He is the same for everyone, offering himself equally for everyone, sacrificing himself equally. For this reason, we may say that in him everyone has come of age, and therewith the distinction between the wise and the immature has ceased. In the days of his flesh he could indeed say: "I thank you, Father, that you have concealed it from the wise and have revealed it to the immature."[5] This could be so, for therein he would have been speaking simply of the empty and false wisdom of this world as he saw it with his own eyes in his own contemporaries.

Through him, however, the immature come of age, as he himself says that he makes them free through truth,[6] for where truth is, there is also maturity of spirit. Thus, there is then no one who could and might elevate oneself above others, for only through him would all be taught by and of God. Further, in this relationship no one would be anything all by oneself. Rather, everyone would receive what is spirit only from the same source, each according to the measure that would be determined by God.

Behold, my Christian listeners, this is the basis, this is the power by virtue of which the Redeemer can and is to abolish inequality among human beings and is to restore true equality among them. Yet, what more are we to say? The cause is there; we must acknowledge it in the one whose birth we celebrate in these days, viewed as the most joyful appearance since the Lord God planted humankind on earth. Yet, how does the result look? Does an equality among human beings then also truly exist through him? Do we still not continually see everywhere, even where the Bible is professed, the same idolatry that some, crawling in the dust, perform before others who are elevated over them by one of those apparent advantages we have noted? By virtue of the same vanity that exists per usual, do we not always still see an externally very important portion among human beings looking down on common people as if these people alone had deteriorated to the null point of earthly life? Those looking down, however, would not necessarily have deteriorated, in that if they wanted to return to the true basis of their customary elevation in society, then they would surely have to recognize themselves as entirely vain and as absolutely nothing. Moreover, this is not only shown in the social life of human beings and in their external relationships. Rather, if we look at the totality of those who profess the name of the Redeemer, how does all that also stand with shared life and activity in the church? To be sure, the Redeemer said to his disciples: "You should not let yourselves

5. Matt 11:25 (NRSV).
6. John 8:32.

be called master; one person is your master, Christ; among one another, however, you are brothers and sisters; and you should call no one father on earth, for the One who is in heaven is your Father."[7]

Yet, what are we hearing? Are there not everywhere individuals who let themselves be called masters, and, to be sure, even masters in Christ, and are they not only too willing to be recognized and honored as such? Further, do not the higher leaders, or directors, of the communities, up to the one who presumes to have to be honored as vicar of Christ, let themselves be called fathers—fathers of faith, venerable fathers, as if the Word in Christ did not exist, the Word that is actually spoken quite directly to and for them? Thus, how far removed would we then be from the fact that the appearance of the Redeemer would have abolished that inequality and would have restored brotherly and sisterly equality on earth! Furthermore, where there is a cause, there also has to be an effect. So accordingly, let us ask, second, how would equality actually be restored through Christ?[8]

II

First, then, what does the apostle mean when he speaks about life in Christ, within the community of persons of faith as such, but then also, second, in many a respect how dubious could it also be for him to seem to speak of this process in relation to our earthly and social relationships? These situations would both be the case, for the first, taken in and of itself alone, my devout listeners, would, to be sure, present no significant difficulty. Why? First, in Christ there would be no inequality, because no comparison would exist, for without comparison, what would the situation of inequality properly claim to mean? If I would not be aware of inequality, if I would not feel that another person stands above me, or that this person's elevation oppresses me, where then would inequality be for me? Likewise, on the other hand, if I myself would not be aware of inequality, if it would not be a matter of my consciousness that I stand

7. Matt 23:9, 10 (NRSV).

8. As indicated in the introduction to this sermon, the first part, then, has been an extension of portions in *Christian Faith* that contribute to an understanding of Christ's person and work as "the basis" for restituting, or restoring, equality among the entirety of humankind. This process is shown, in particular, by Schleiermacher's employing key examples afresh here. The "how" of the matter, to be shown in the second section, can be expected to bear the same characteristics (*Christian Faith*, §§92–112).

above another person, then inequality would also not be in me. Rather, I might well, indeed, put myself on a par with any other person. However, in Christ there would be no comparison and, therefore, also no inequality, for it would not be a Christian work, my devout listeners, if we should compare ourselves with each other so as to take our own measure in our life with Christ. Only children put measure and weight on what they have received and, accordingly, consider themselves either superior or inferior. Moreover, the same thing would indeed then be the case with us as well, for in what would we mostly take delight, each one viewing it in some other? What would we be especially inclined to admire, each one in the other? Indeed, the answer is simply that which a human being is by the help of God, thus we would admire that which has been received! We would rejoice with such pleasure inasmuch as God's grace would be powerful in those who would otherwise have been weak. We would prefer to admire this effect if the divine Spirit in its leading some among us from one degree of clarity to another for the benefit of everyone were also lifting for review any frailty of the human spirit. Moreover, if we should look at another person and rejoice in this person, and if we should do this with the spirit of brotherly and sisterly love, then, at the same time, we would not be looking strictly at ourselves or asking whether within us there is more or less of this same divine gift. We would be rejoicing in Christ as we do in certain others and we would be beholding Christ in them, and precisely this beholding of Christ in other human beings would be filling our entire existence in such a moment, with the result that we would know nothing further regarding ourselves!

On the other hand, if, at some other time, we would be looking at ourselves, the question arises: Should we really do this? Indeed we should, my devout friends. Yet, then we should be truly looking simply at ourselves and not at others; then we should certainly be comparing ourselves but not with others or in accordance with some merely human measure, for the later occurrence would give the lazy heart simply an opportunity for a thousand excuses to arise. Instead, we should be comparing ourselves solely with the Redeemer himself. We would be measuring ourselves over against the Redeemer, but then we would not be asking how much divine life other persons have already absorbed, whether it is more or less. Rather, we would have to ask only whether we too have truly devoted ourselves to him, whether there is a community of life between him and us! Properly speaking, the existence of this very community is itself a subject for gratitude without measure, and we have simply to measure in ourselves whether or not we have improved in it and how. Thus, there is then no comparison between one of us and others, and where there is no comparison, there is no inequality. Thus, in the true life of Christians as such, as they have become brothers and sisters through him and have received from him alone the power to be children of God, inequality has always been abolished already, because all occasions that would tend to observe any inequality would be lacking!

Likewise, on the other hand, there can be no inequality where no one can be strictly segregated and separated from another, and it is like this among Christians. They are not only like one another, viewed as many persons, but, the apostle has said, they are all one in Christ. No one can separate oneself entirely from any of the rest, in such a way that one would engage or confront others simply for oneself. No one can be something without the others, and the others cannot be something without each given person. Consider the following two statements of the apostle: First, that which we read here in our text: "You are all one in Christ"; and, second, that which he says on another occasion: "Let no one boast concerning a human being, thus, no one may say, 'I belong to Peter, I to Paul. Rather, all things are yours."[9] These two statements thus essentially belong together. This is so, for among Christians everything is one shared life and activity, one shared work and one shared possession, and precisely on that account also one shared merit and one shared fault, or guilt! For this reason, where there is no separation, there is also no inequality. Yet, to be sure, suppose that this unholy spirit of separation, of wanting to be something for oneself alone, if this most conceited arrogance of the human mind and heart should begin to get control of minds and hearts again, and in such a way that the two conditions arise, namely, separation and comparison. Then, discord would also enter in, and at that point the beautiful work of the Redeemer would begin to unravel. Where he is, there is this equality without which alone that separation of which we spoke cannot exist. Where his love holds sway, where the single rule he left for his own is followed (namely, that among ourselves we love one another with the love with which he has loved us)is then exemplified—oh, then no reflection on any inequality would exist, and no consciousness of any more or less would exist. Rather, the equality of a blessed peace is simply there.

9. 1 Cor 3:22.

However, now let us also ask the question: How do things stand with respect to this work of the Redeemer if we should now look at the totality of human relationships? We ask this, for, as the apostle says, we should indeed not want to move out of this world. Rather, the reign of God is to be founded in this world, and we truly are unable to separate precisely that spiritual existence, that inner divine life, from the manifold works to which each person is called in this world, based on those orders under the sole protection of which these works can succeed. Now, if we ask in what manner is equality then restored here, then, for the same reason, to be sure, we must reflect on what I already previously called to mind, namely, that divine life is not innate in anyone among us. However much one may be born and raised within the pale of the Christian church, each person must, first of all, always especially acquire divine life. Faith must become an active occurrence in a person's mind and heart, and with it divine life must begin in each person. Further, for each person there was a time when one was first prepared for this life except when divine life appeared, and then one's calling came to be clear to oneself.

Further, now let us also consider another saying of the apostle:[10] "Let everyone remain in the calling to which one is called. If you are a slave, remain a slave, but know that you are a free person in Christ." Therewith, however, the apostle has also said: "If in the meantime you can come to be free, make use of it more willingly. If a slave is a free person in Christ, then equality is indeed restored," away from a situation of inequality. Yet, this saying of the apostle is not, as it were, applicable solely to this particular relationship! This is the case, for the apostle who said: "You are one in Christ," also saw and grasped this equality in the totality of human relationships. He did so even if, at that time, he still had no occasion to speak of it, because the gospel had not yet permeated through to the nobles and rulers of the earth.

Yet, on what is everything then based here? Is it not based on the orders of human society? However, the apostle envisages these orders as a divine work when he says that authorities are appointed by God. Thus, in his view, if one is called to be a ruler, then one may also remain in this calling. This applies to any one ruler as well as it does to another! Just as he said that the authorities are appointed by God and bear the sword of justice for the protection of what is good against what is evil,[11] so too

---

10. 1 Cor 7:20–22.

11. Rom 13:1–4.

all the rulers on earth who have prestige also have to be conscious of having no inequality before their brothers and sisters with respect to the Lord—all the more so when they use the proper measure and protect that which is proper and good to protect. This is so, for if they are placed for the protection of good persons, they serve these persons and are so completely conscious of their proper relationships to their brothers and sisters that they can and must also perfectly apply to themselves what the Redeemer himself says of himself, namely, that he came to serve, and that if someone wants to be the most prominent, may this person serve the others.

Accordingly, consider the following statement of the apostle: "But if you can come to be free, make use of it more willingly."[12] This statement is also not said to the slaves alone. No, it applies to authorities and nobles just as well as to those of humble birth. This is so, for truly what can be more oppressive for a mind and heart enlightened by God and thus also conscious of recognizing the equality of all human beings—human beings who stand before the One whose throne is in heaven, and human beings who live in this community of the Redeemer on earth, and who foster this community—each member as best one can? What, I say, can be more oppressive for such a person than when this person becomes aware that a false feeling of inequality still influences the life of human-kind, and that for this reason a timid submissiveness holds back many fine forces from properly exercised free efficacy in service of spiritual life? For this reason, this statement also applies to them! To them it is also said: If you can come to be free of such a burden, make use of it more willingly! If you believe that the time has come to stretch just a bit these constricting barriers that separate you from your brothers and sisters in many a diverse manner, or if you believe the time has come to demolish these barriers here and there and to bring your brothers and sisters closer to you, oh, then do use this opportunity more willingly!

Should we want to deny, or could we deny, moreover, that this decrease of inequality is a blessed work, one that would advance ever farther from one time to the next among Christian peoples? Regarding the relationship between masters and slaves, for example, how has it been mitigated over the course of time! Also, how much latitude of con-sciousness has already been found among us of a brotherly and sisterly equality—among both those who rule in household affairs and those who

12. 1 Cor 7:21.

serve? Further, regarding that large gap between the power that gives and upholds laws and those who follow and obey them, how far has that gap not already been filled? The force of Christian humility does not cease teaching that in matters of this world even wisdom is not innate in anyone, and no one person alone is the bearer of wisdom. This would be the case, for it indeed follows from all these considerations that the more each person requires of wisdom to fill the position allotted to anyone by God worthily, the more diligently this person also has to look around for wisdom and to draw to oneself those with whom one can find wisdom. Now, if even in civil life what is truly good, and if a uniformly, widely held satisfaction can be caused only by such a union among persons, then all human strengths and virtues that contribute to civil life must also find their acknowledgment therein, provided that those who are called to the management of matters human are able to render before God a joyful account of what has been entrusted to them! If, however, everything good is valued in this way and not in accordance with the place from which good comes but in accordance with its efficacy, then any inequality must become ever more meaningless![13]

Matters proceed in this way among Christian peoples, and they should proceed in this way from one generation to the next. Moreover, if ever a time should return when human order would be dissolved around us, and thereby composure and peace would be endangered even for us Christians, then the higher spiritual power that we owe to the gospel and the purer, brotherly and sisterly love that Christianity would have planted in us would have developed into a means for our protection and our preservation. Moreover, in their fruits we will then know with grateful joy that in truth the Redeemer also came to abolish inequality and its unfortunate consequences through the fact that it is he alone who stands equally above everyone.

Accordingly, may he be welcomed and celebrated as such by us anew, in that he was not ashamed to call us brothers and sisters! As we are now all equal among one another, because we can only be something

13. This discourse on inequality and equality both offers an extrapolation upon his *Christian Faith* and provides a bridge carried emotionally to his *Christian Ethics*. The latter function represents an extension from his earlier focus on life within the church to households and to social, civil, and political life. To get a good start within this arena, one consistent with the analysis given here, see his *Christian Household* sermons (1820, 1826; ET: Seidel and Tice, *The Christian Household*) and consider Theodore Vial's interpretations of Schleiermacher's considerable, principled approach to civil and political life in Vial, *Schleiermacher* (2013), 101–17.

through him, so it is his imparting love that wants to draw us all up to him, just as it keeps us together among one another and bears the life of each one of us. Further, if he calls us brothers and sisters, this is the assurance that through him and like him we also have the same community with him and with our Father in heaven.[14] Amen.

14. Unquestionably, the final Christmas sermon (or 1833) also builds on the 1832 sermon and includes an interpretation of other annual festival sermons in relation to that at Christmas. It also includes three features worth noting in advance: (1) In its discussion and use of Scripture, a foretaste of how he would have designed a further revised Introduction to Christian Faith, possibly even a joint edition of that work and of his Christian Ethics (the two aspects of dogmatics), which he knew he would not live long enough to accomplish; (2) a refined exploration of issues regarding the appropriations of God's love and grace in celebration of Christmas and issuing experiences of joy at Easter and Pentecost as well; and (3) psychological and sociological complements to earlier examinations of individual and communal experiences of Christian faith and life, respectively, approaches that mark his analyses as far advanced beyond both fields, which scarcely even existed at that time.

11

How Exactly Our Festive Christmas Joy Coincides with the Faith that Jesus Is God's Son, Who Is the Victory That Overcomes the World

Second Day of Christmas
Thursday, December 26, 1833[1]

Who is it that conquers [overcomes] the world
but the one who believes [has faith] that Jesus is the Son of God?
—1 JOHN 5:5 (NRSV)

My devout listeners, in our Christian congregations it is a fixed and well-established arrangement that some designated word of Holy Scripture is always foundational to our devout reflection. So too, it is natural that, given the great number of subjects for the pious thoughts of Christians and given the small number of our New Testament writings, there would be very different ways to treat words of Holy Scripture precisely as they bear upon our Christian sermons. Sometimes it is quite actually the word of Scripture itself, in accordance with its more exact content and in its various references, that directs the thoughts of the speaker, who then also attracts the attention of listeners to the same Word. In contrast, sometimes it also happens that, by some particular aspect of what it contains

---

1. This revised sermon, preached on Thursday, December 26, 1833, first appeared in a local, limited edition (1834), 215–35, then in SW II.3 (1835), 738–51, and (1843), 763–76.

when a word of Scripture is read aloud, that aspect becomes an occasion to explicate certain thoughts from it that, to be sure, have to be important for our purposes at this location. Moreover, no more fault is to be assigned to the second way than to the first.

Likewise, in our own religious gatherings there is also a twofold way to celebrate our Christian festivals. Sometimes it is quite actually the subject of the festival to which we attach ourselves with song, prayer, and public discourse. On the other hand, sometimes it also happens that the event that is actually being celebrated likewise serves more as motivation, in order not to enjoin on Christians both a particular element of a text itself and some element that is a necessary ingredient in any one of its essential relations. In that many among you, my devout friends, are no doubt repeating to yourselves the words of Scripture read aloud today, these persons could also readily believe the following. That is, if in these words the immediate subject of our festival, namely, the birth of the Lord, would actually not be the subject at all, my discourse today might also diverge along this second path, in regard both to the content of the text and the use that I intend to make of the text, also to the handling of today's festival as well. However, I am not taking this path. Rather, my actual intention is to present to you how our festive Christmas joy exactly coincides with the fact that, as our text says, the faith that Jesus is God's Son is the victory that conquers, or overcomes, the world.

I

Now, let us suppose that initially we must consider how precisely this faith is the actual subject of our Christian joy, namely, that in Jesus the Son of God is born to us. Then, in general terms, first of all, let us together look at everything that in our daily domestic and civic life is similar to this festival. As Scripture says, when a woman is about to give birth, she has pain, but when she has given birth, her anxiety ceases and gives way to the joy that someone is born to the light of day.[2] Now, this would be a beautiful expression of the inner gratitude of our hearts toward God, when in the domestic circle we celebrate the day that is marked by the birth of one of our children. Likewise, however, in reverse and with

---

2. John 16:21. In Schleiermacher's *Christmas Eve Celebration* (1806; ET: Tice, 2010), the women gathered in the domestic circle depicted there first offer stories from their lives, including the story of a birth, before the men within the circle introduce a set of interpretive accounts.

sincere gratitude, children also celebrate the day when God allowed their parents to be born for them, the parents to whom they themselves owe their very lives and at whose hand they wander along the path of life in most intimate company. Each child attains the same joy; the joy over one's being born into the light of day, as one whom God has placed near to us, viewed as a special subject of our love and concern. However, let us also look at broader and larger circles!

Suppose that there are individuals who are situated and endowed by God in such a way that they can well deserve approval from human society, given their services, of whatever kind they may be. Suppose too that these services for many whose well-being depends on the undisturbed continuation of their effective actions, are bound up in the life and activity of these individuals. Indeed, even when this is not the case, but an even purer and more spiritual participation in the existence of another person rests not simply on what someone has already done or will still do but rests quite actually on what that very person is to us in our proceeding from admiration of what has a beautiful form, under which the human spirit does occasionally appear on earth. Each type, those who are excellent benefactors of human society and those who by their very existence shine in an extraordinary manner, is honored by many in the same way. Indeed, there are even individual cases where this process lasts not only for the time in which such persons live, but extends long after they have already passed away from the entire generation that personally enjoyed their association, and their effect is still celebrated with the same gratitude on a special day, itself viewed as a beautiful festival of joyful remembrance. Yet, how long might this remembrance last? How long could it last, given the swift course of human affairs? It lasts as long as human memory can last, according to the usual meaning of the word. That is, it can last until the second or third generation, whose members can still view, at least in their childhoods, the outstanding individuals honored in this way. Beginning beyond that point, however, is a forgetfulness of every immediate connection that many would be able to make with the life of such an individual. Beyond that point, everything passes on simply as noteworthy instances within the general and particular histories of human beings.

Now, we may then ask: How much does the celebration of these days of Christmas differ from any other celebration of this kind? What general participation in it would we actually desire? How is it still not enough that only such and such a part of humankind actually celebrates with us the Redeemer's appearance on earth! How would we indeed want that much more and much farther everything that breathes in the life of the light and of the Spirit would share this joy with us more broadly and fully! How would we indeed detect that everyone would be ever more sure of its grounding within their inner being!

Meanwhile, I would also not want to conceal anything that exists on the other side of this matter. Christian communities do exist, indeed numerous ones, that observe this beautiful festival just as markedly little as they observe our other great Christian celebrations. However, they do not neglect it because, as it were, they have believed any less that Jesus of Nazareth was born as God's Son or have rejoiced any less in that [faith, or] belief. Rather, wholly at one with us in this belief, they would simply tend to proceed based on the fact that precisely because this faith or belief comes from on high, because it points to something of a divine notion, consciousness of it and joy in it should not also be subject to the changes and variability of what is merely earthly. They would require that the deepest and innermost feeling of gratitude for the Redeemer's appearance should not be tied to particular designated days and, in this way, come to be known only in such particular days. Rather, they might hold that we should always be full of this joy in the same way. Every shared reflection on the cherished truths of our faith, every shared awakening to hope and love toward the one in whom we have faith and believe should include this same joy, the same consciousness of everything great and divine, from his initial beginning until his final great work, all of which involved an outpouring of the divine Spirit.

Still, on the other side of this matter, but even more, there are also many individual Christians, both among us now just as they were elsewhere at all previous times, who would indeed have belonged to the community of faith and would celebrate precisely this festival with us in true joy and heartfelt gratitude. Yet, suppose that we asked them: Is the reason for your joy truly the same for you and is the subject of this festival, namely, that Jesus is born the Son of God, also the same for you? Then, some would be rather uncertain about affirming this, and some would prefer to express their denial directly. Thereby many of them would surely be of the most creditable opinion. It would seem to them as if those who first smoothed the way toward putting into words that inexhaustible feeling of adoration toward the one whom God had sent— a feeling originally indwelling within persons of faith—that those who were to present this subject in such a way that everyone could profess the same things, had not always gone to work with the greatest discernment, perhaps also not always with the most exact and reliable acquaintance with human language. They might well believe that all those wretched quarrels about such subjects among Christians originated precisely from this process. Furthermore, on this account it might be better to be satisfied with expressions from them that have not been capable of such easy misinterpretation but are, at the same time, easy for everyone to understand. Moreover, even if the expressions chosen would not exalt the Redeemer to the same height of what might be deemed miraculous already from the beginning of his existence, they would, nonetheless, present the nature of faith in him properly and purely. We do not want to condemn those people! Just suppose that they might. Suppose that they hesitated to agree with the words of our text because they supposed that a time would come when human beings would have drawn long enough from the as yet unknown source that Jesus could not open up for them, and because they already had come to settle under the new light that Jesus of Nazareth himself had not yet seen. Then, in this way a time would come when even Christ would be replaced more fully (with respect to his services within human thoughts and feelings), in that with full hearts they would be turning toward this greater thing that God would have given them. For them, this would be the right time—just as would be true for us, given the light of the New Testament, regarding revelations that writings within the still older Old Testament might contain—when the writings of the New Testament would likewise step further into the background. If this, I say, would be their reasoning, then, to be sure, their acknowledgment of Christ would be quite remote from ours.

However, stemming from both kinds of deviations, from the first no less than from the second, we do indeed see how true it is that the subject of our joy is simply the birth of Jesus, the Son of God. That is to say, the first group demands that the feelings of our heart should be so completely steady and that our consciousness of the Redeemer should be so continuous and selfsame throughout life, precisely because they would know that this consciousness came from above and would have what is divine both in reason and for its object. Moreover, precisely the second group would want to move beyond our celebration and joy, because they would not acknowledge the process of consciousness that we might actually possess, viewed by them as having occurred and being sufficient for its own reasons. Yet, precisely by their not wanting to join in our celebration, they would indeed express for us who take part in this process and desire that until the day comes when, in accordance with the wish of the first group, we will have passed over from what is variable into what is invariable and then would thus always celebrate the entire life of the Redeemer on a regular basis. We can want the celebration only because, in fact, between Jesus Christ and all others is such a difference with respect to God's grace and divine mercy, a difference that we can describe only in a way that Scripture—notably the words of our text, the words of the disciple John, whom the Lord especially loved—describes him throughout.

Yet, to be sure, how we would ruin this beautiful festival of joy if we then wanted to put this expression on the level of human sophistry. That is to say, suppose that we then wanted to be absorbed more closely in such designations of human dogmatic wisdom—designations that may or may not encompass our devotion to the newborn Jesus. No, so that we may arrive at a proper consciousness regarding this expression, let us rather consider words of Scripture that intend to designate precisely its actual and true content.

Accordingly, let us compare what the author of the Letter to the Hebrews says: That we had to have a high priest, who would be holy, undefiled, and set apart from sinners.[3] Oh, my devout friends, suppose that something really does exist that could bring such a sad tone even into our Christmas joy, even inasmuch as this joy would be directed to Jesus, the Son of God. To be sure, many pious conditions of a Christian mind and heart do bear this sad tone within themselves. Then, this sad feature would lie precisely in that we are acquainted with it so definitively and have become aware of it in our innermost being, namely: No one who was not holy from the very beginning on would come to be holy, and no one who was not undefiled from the beginning on could be set apart from sinners. If we then must have such a high priest, he would have had to be so far above other human beings—though partaking of the same human nature—that he would have been holy from the very beginning on, he would have been undefiled in his entire course of life through this sinful world; and thus, walking in the midst of sinners, loving sinners, and affecting sinners with all the strengths of his spirit, he would, nonetheless, have remained set apart from sinners, as set apart as heaven is from earth. Indeed, there can be even more, for the same author adds that we had to have such a high priest, viewed as one who is higher than the heavens!

3. Heb 7:26.

Moreover, when John the Baptist was fulfilling the greatest and most significant action of his life, which was likewise especially blessed by God, and when Jesus of Nazareth came to be baptized by him, a voice came to him from heaven, a voice that said: "This is my beloved Son, in whom I am well pleased."[4] God cannot be well pleased in face of sin. God cannot be well pleased in face of anything that is nugatory within itself and empty. Yes, God can be well pleased only in face of Godself and in face of what is directly from God! Thus, these two things are also simply one and the same. That is to say: Consider what that voice expressed, namely, that he is my beloved Son; indeed even more, that he is my own Son, and he is the one in whom I am well pleased—truly, purely, serenely, and mixed with nothing else! If we combine these two thoughts, if thereby we imbue ourselves precisely with the consciousness that where sin once is, also bears its effects and coexists, it would never again be permissible that a person would be completely set apart from it. For precisely this reason, it would also never be permissible that something's being strictly from God would be well pleasing to God if it were a defiled object. Oh, we will indeed have to speak in this way. This is so, for the one who was nonetheless set apart there would be no designation other than the one that Scripture has conveyed as it has selected, and of which the apostle John has also availed himself in our text!

Yes, often Scripture also indicates this view of the Redeemer in another way. When the Lord God had made all things and looked at them, the Lord God said that everything was good.[5] Thus, God was well pleased with the world, the same world in which soon thereafter sin was indeed alive and was effective, the same world in which deviations from the pure and holy divine will were multiplying! However, for precisely this reason, Scripture also says that the Redeemer, the Son of God, through whom God has addressed us in recent days, is the one who bears all things. The Redeemer bears the world in such a way that it remains an object of God's being well pleased. Only because the Redeemer exists and is effective in the world can the world be an object of God's being well pleased. Accordingly, we will thus have to say that precisely the birth of the Redeemer that designates for us—as we can indeed grasp everything in an earthly way only in a series composed of a temporal development of all things human, of all spiritual life that is actually known to us, hence the return

---

4. Matt 3:17; Mark 1:11; Luke 3:22.
5. Gen 1:31.

to communion with God during the appearance of the one who lived and was effective as the Son of God on earth.

However, precisely inasmuch as Jesus, viewed as the Son of God, is now the subject of our festive joy on this day and inasmuch as we know this, only on this basis can we then have faith, or believe, that we too please God again through him and are pleasing to God in God's Son. This is so, if in this way he was the pure subject of what is God's being well pleased, if in this way he was the consummate, prototypical image[6] of the divine being and the reflection of God's glory. Moreover, we would want to trace our joy in his existence and efficacy to his birth, precisely because from his birth on he had to be holy, undefiled, and set apart from sinners. Indeed, just for this reason, we would also certainly not want to stop celebrating this beautiful festival with one another until we should attain to this perfection, until the entire world should be permeated by him, and by his life, and, in this way until he should return again to the world, itself viewed as pleasing to God, since God created it. On the other hand, we would indeed also have to say—and it is this that we want to consider in the second part of our reflection—that the content of this joy is likewise the victory that overcomes the world.

II

However, that I present this theme almost immediately after what I simply stated, namely, that the world is a subject of God's being well-pleased in and by the Son of God, on this occasion, to be sure, it would especially have had to strike me how the expressions of Scripture, in the way they are also included in our overall Christian language, often contradict each other in a very apparent manner. The world is well pleasing to God because it is God's work, and the world is itself to be overcome. At the same time, the person who overcomes the world says of himself that he came not to judge the world but to make it holy. Hence, the same world that is to be overcome is also to be made holy. Further, if he says that he did not come to judge the world, he indeed also says, at the same time, that the person who does not have faith, or believe, in him is already judged.[7] So, it indeed remains to be noted that the world is to be judged. That is,

6. To catch Schleiermacher's meaning of the "image" in his own terms, *consummate* and *prototypical* are added here.

7. John 5:19–30.

the world is to be both overcome and judged. It is thereby to be made holy and to be made an object of God's being well pleased. So, we ask: How can all this be combined in one and the same subject? Moreover, if it cannot be combined, how vexing would the language of our faith then be in its confounding by application of the same word and in its mingling among each other different things which were supposed to be carefully kept separated from each other but are confused, in that they are actually contrary to each other? Nonetheless, however, this complaint would not be properly lodged here, for the situation is to be viewed in this way and in no other way. It is the same world that is made holy and the same world that is overcome; it is the same world that is judged and the same world that is led back to God's being well pleased. Yet, we must ask: How so?

Throughout, my devout friends, on consideration of all matters human, insofar as they belong to our spiritual life, ultimately we return to a great contrast over and against which we would also constantly measure and evaluate everything human. The one aspect is the divine, the true, the essential one; the other aspect is the nugatory, the pernicious, that which opposes the first aspect. The first aspect, however, is only God in Godself and what is from God, and it is thus also propagated everywhere in accordance with divine omnipresence. The second aspect, however, we do indeed find everywhere in this our world but only in the manner of what is empty and nugatory, and especially wherever an individual's sensory nature, which is well known to us, dominates. Thus, to be sure, the world contains what is nugatory and pernicious, what within itself struggles against what is true and essential, yet it does so as that which is to be overcome and ultimately destroyed. However, the divine, which is in the world, that which God communicated to a human being when God placed him as lord of the earth, and which is now not only being restored but is being established in the one who is the image of the divine Being in a far higher manner than what existed when he appeared, is this divine creation not to remain empty and alone? No, instead this particular divine creation is to gain control over all the strengths of human nature, in which the world itself is also implicated; it is to hold sway over and have an effect on everything by means of human nature, and this is precisely the same world that is to be made holy and is to stand again as the subject of God's being well pleased in the most intimate communion with God and by means of the one who is the image of God's Being. Thus, to be overcome and judged includes everything that is nugatory in itself, everything that struggles against what is true and divine, everything that comes merely from what is transitory and that coincides with it, and (to the extent that it has power and holds sway and has an effect) is also in position to drag what is higher and divine into what is transitory. This is the world that is to be both destroyed and judged.

However, insofar as precisely this human nature, or precisely this earthly existence, is itself capable of being controlled, ensouled and permeated by what is divine, this is the very world that is to be blessed, the world in which God is revealed evermore and in that world, inasmuch as it is to become perfect, is to be known and can be known and seen exactly as we know and see God now in God's Son, who is the source of this gradual restoration, indeed glorification, of the world.

Yet, we do not know that the world is overcome and judged in order to be blessed as something already finished. The world is viewed even now only as a matter continuing still. This is so, for although we know, and can attest it to ourselves with truth, that the old human being dies even as soon as we are born from God, by means of faith in Jesus himself viewed as the Son of God.[8] Moreover, although it is true that the old human being dies away, the consequences of one's old life do indeed still continue on in our lives, though what is divine does grasp hold of a person evermore. What is nugatory and pernicious always comes about again, as often as a person—to be sure, viewed as one who also bears what is divine within oneself—is born again unto the light of the earthly world! Throughout, the world that has to be overcome does reappear, with the result that the new world that is blessed and in which divine love shines may be born from within it!

Suppose, however, that we now ask how our part in overcoming of the world is proceeding, and how even if it is taken to be such a constantly continuing work, this overcoming is to be merged with a celebration like today's—one that attaches to and merges into definitely specified times, also in such a way that the overcoming is to be the subject and content of the celebration. In that light, let me first take notice of the process of overcoming.

What we know as such a continuing work of God is also one of which we become aware within ourselves as the never ending conflict between spirit and flesh. What is then actually the object of every brotherly and sisterly fusion of our strengths and of all communal Christian doings and action on earth—namely, that we everywhere both contest

8. John 3:3–8.

and seek to overcome the nugatory things of the world and to overcome their nature and work, and we also do this so as to form and to expand the reign of God. We view this divinely led process, to be sure, as a communal work of God within and among us, and this is the content of our total activity inasmuch as it is from God. Yet, suppose that we stop at some point to reflect on what we are doing and how we are doing it, and also to reflect on this work of God and on how it happens. Then, on what do our glances fall, to what does our spiritual eye turn other than to Jesus, the Son of God from the beginning of his earthly life on? Accordingly, precisely the consciousness of this continuing overcoming of the world, as we bring it to clarity within ourselves, becomes for us nothing other than joy over the coming of Jesus, the Son of God. This is so, for it was in this place and with this first moment of his appearance that the victory he was to accomplish began. Before that moment there could be no comparable acquaintance within a human heart with this overcoming. Instead, any anticipation of it would have existed only as a dim presentiment of things to come.

In contrast, consider the other question regarding how the overcoming of the world happens. Here again we are in the same situation, one in which seemingly contradictory expressions of Scripture occur to each observer. In our text the apostle says: Who overcomes the world other than the one who has faith, or believes, that Jesus is the Son of God? Thus, in this way he envisages this conquering, or overcoming, of the world as our work, at least as the work of our faith. However, the Redeemer says to his disciples, and this disciple too had heard and had reported it, namely: In the world, you have fear, but be of good hope, for "I have overcome the world."[9] Accordingly, he presents as his own work the same matter that is presented here by his disciple as our work and specifically the work of our faith. The two other sources, my devout friends, are indeed simply one and the same. If we properly understand our celebration today, how it leads us to the birth, to the first appearance of the Redeemer in the world, and yet has as its subject nothing other than precisely this, that he is the Son of God, it is indeed obvious that, on that ground alone, we might disregard everything that the Redeemer actually did, for at this time he had not yet done anything. Further, in the way he existed when he first appeared, inactive, yet to take in everything

9. John 16:33 (NRSV).

that was gradually to emerge from him, he would still be the subject of our confession of faith and of this festival.

If this surprises us, well then let us ask: When the Lord says, I have overcome the world, is there then some particular deed of the Redeemer or several deeds, or is it, as it were, the totality of his deeds to which he is referring? To be sure, we are quite accustomed—as then even Holy Scripture itself precedes us therein, given its own example, and no one will want to have any objection to this—we are accustomed to include all the Redeemer's efficacious action in his obedience until its very peak at his death on the cross, in the surrender of his life for the life of humankind. Yet, he spoke those words before he had arrived at this peak of his activity. Indeed, even if, disregarding this fact, we should want to ask whether precisely the Redeemer's death brought about the overcoming of the world. Then, if we want to characterize it literally, precisely this victory would no longer have to be a continuing work of God. Rather, it would be what happened once and for all. We would have nothing more to do thereby and would already have been standing, for a very long time, as victors in the world's overcoming.

Suppose that we embrace what the Redeemer did, insofar as we can include even his death and his suffering, viewed, on the other hand, as the deed of his obedience—oh, how little, how isolated, how disconnected that one deed would be! How little would truly have been accomplished when he said, it is finished! How little of what we actually call his works and deeds precisely with respect to his purifying the world, to his founding and building of God's reign, would he have done by then! Instead, the situation was really like this: He did not overcome the world simply by what he did; rather, he was overcoming it by what he was then and continued to do! Precisely because he would have been effecting all of this overcoming by what he is, inasmuch as he would also be recognized for this, at the same time, because all his individual deeds, all his individual works, would be nothing compared with that of his actual obedience, which was his constant work but which we tend not to call either a work or a deed in the narrower and usual meaning of these words—that is, in that he bore witness to himself, in that just as he gave himself up he also pronounced and declared how he alone was one with his Father—yes, precisely for these reasons there would be no contradiction between his own word and that of his disciple in our text. In comparison with these utterances of Christ about himself, in comparison with his constantly bearing witness regarding himself, he made himself known to humankind as he in his truth and love, as the true divine image. In comparison with all these self-ascriptions, all of his works and deeds that we can actually name as such would come across as simply nothing. However, he was also that image only inasmuch as giving this witness included a force that human beings could not evade, and indeed a force that in human beings themselves, in turn, would became the power to live as God's children, at the same time. Actually, he would have done nothing strictly definite and particular; rather, as John the Evangelist says: His entire life lay simply in the fact that there appeared in him and from him the glory of the only begotten Son of the Father, full of grace and truth, making itself known, also in the fact that precisely this mode of being compelled human beings to insistent acknowledgment precisely of this glory. By this process, those who received him at that time and in this way, who did not belong to the darkness that shut him out and that rejected him—though even this darkness was to be illuminated by him—did then receive the strength to be God's children. Hence, in truth it makes no difference whether the Redeemer says: "I have overcome the world," or whether his disciple reports this of him.[10] John, to whom it probably never occurred to want to match wits with the person beside whom he was accustomed to rest, says in our text: Our faith is the victory that overcomes the world.[11] This would be so, for whoever overcomes the world besides simply one who has faith in Jesus as the Son of God? So, in fact, the two are one and the same! By our faith the Son of God overcomes the world, and our faith overcomes the world by and through him, by and through his divine force or strength, just as our faith is nothing but the continuation of his force, or strength, and his life in us, the hope in which we take pride that we share in all his deeds, does indeed occur in likeness to him and in a relationship to God as children, by and through him!

Behold, my good friends, if here, at the first beginning of our church year, we bring together the entire series of festivals that belong to our principal Christian festival, we will have to admit that each one holds its particular place, none is to be preferred to another or is inferior to another. Each one, however, has its special time in which it prevails over the others. So, the festival of Christ's resurrection could be nowhere more splendid than that which celebrates the first beginnings of the Christian

10. John 16:33.

11. 1 John 5:4. The NRSV speaks of "our faith" as something that "conquers the world." The preferable word "overcomes" has also been used elsewhere in this context, as it is elsewhere in the NRSV.

church. Moreover, however splendidly and joyfully we might celebrate it even now, naturally our celebration of it does not come up to how this resurrection event was always present to people in the initial proclamation of the Lord's apostles. Each word that they proclaimed was also of nothing but a celebration of a new Easter. Christ has arisen! We see how this lay out the soul of their spirit, and we see how after his death his glory would have arisen for them anew therein. As they themselves said: They also wanted to be nothing but witnesses of his resurrection, and their entire life and activity was a continuing Easter. Moreover, when we think of the spread of the Christian church outward, we see how one people after another has been gripped by the truth of the divine Word and of the tidings that the Son of God was born and broke the force of sin and restored the peace that comes from God. When we consider how the apostles themselves have commented on all this and in effect say: Faith comes from the sermon, but the sermon comes from the Word of God;[12] as the Spirit has given it to the apostles to express, we will have to say this: Wherever we observe this effect of Christianity on humankind, there Pentecost is celebrated. This living consciousness of the divine Spirit and of its efficacy in instruments that, to be sure, are also weakened by sin, for since the Redeemer is no longer physically present on earth, there is no longer any other kind of instrument. In contrast, a consciousness of effects wrought by the divine Spirit, effects that distinguish it from all other simply human wisdom, which has not been able to bring human beings together and encompass them within a reign of God, this has unmistakably been the ongoing event of Pentecost. Moreover, as long as this work of the dissemination of Christianity will continue, it will move persons of faith as a Pentecost event does. Consider our calm, peaceful life in the midst of the Christian church, viewed as our fine and humble destiny. However, what is this other than that we are at work overcoming the world, first each of us within ourselves but then also among everyone with whom we are connected by the bond of love and friendship—an overcoming of the world ever more in our entire broader public life, just as in this shared, undisturbed development of our existence we reflect on ourselves with the aim of gaining surety regarding ourselves. What would we then be celebrating other than the beautiful festival of Christmas ever anew? Consider our joy in everything that the Redeemer does with us and by means of us. What, in fact, would this joy be but joy in him, in

12. Rom 10:17.

the fact that he, the Son of God, was born and lived for our sakes, that the eternal Word has become flesh among us, and in consequence there is also joy in his overall appearance on earth and in the image that was established by him among us that has become for us a source of blessedness, or salvation, as well as the source of our faith and of the activity of faith through love! Accordingly, let us also gladly acknowledge that it is indeed a fine festival which recurs every year for our delight. It has its truth and meaning, however, only in this ever-continuing work, simply by the fact that we celebrate it anew each time as often as we become aware of our relationship to the Redeemer, and also simply by the fact that when we speak with one another out of the fullness of our hearts, we always remember anew that it is the Savior of the world who was born, Jesus who appeared, as the Son of God!

So, ever more let us hold firm in him the designation that we have received through him of becoming children of God, that it may also be our faith that is ever more overcoming the world and subjects the world to his sway, this in order that every knee may bow before him who is Lord over all that is human. Amen.

Bibliography

Works by and on Schleiermacher

Schleiermacher, Friedrich. "Address Celebrating the Third Centennial of the Reformation of the Church by Luther held at the University of Berlin held on 3 November, 1817." Tice, ET of his *Oratio*, in *Friedrich Schleiermacher on Creeds, Confessions and Church Union: That They May Be One*, translated, with an introduction and notes by Iain G. Nicol, 45–64. Translated, with an introduction and notes by Iain G. Nicol. Schleiermacher Studies and Translations 24. Lewiston: Mellen, 2004.

———. *Brief Outline of Theology as a Field of Study* (1811 & 1830 editions). 3rd ed. and revised translation by Terrence N. Tice. Louisville: Westminster John Knox, 2011. xxi + 191 pp.

———. *Christian Faith: A New Translation and Critical Edition.* 2 vols. Edited by Catherine L. Kelsey and Terrence N. Tice. Translated by Terrence N. Tice et al. 2 vols. Louisville: Westminster John Knox, 2016. xxix + 1140 pp.

———. *The Christian Household: A Sermonic Treatise.* Translated with essays and notes by Dietrich Seidel and Terrence N. Tice. Schleiermacher Studies and Translations 3. Lewiston, NY: Mellen, 1991. xli + 237 pp.

———. *Christliche Festpredigten und Predigten in Bezug auf die Feier der Ubergabe der Augsburgischen Confession (1826, 1831).* SW II.2. Berlin: Reimer, 1834, 1843; *Predigten Fünfte bis Siebente Sammlung (1826-1833).* KGA III.2. Berlin: de Gruyter, 2016. liii + 1220 pp.

———. *Christliche Sittenlehre* (Vorlesung im Wintersemeter 1826/27). Edited by Hermann Peiter. Berlin: Lit, 2011. 635 pp.

———. *Christmas Eve Celebration: A Dialogue; A Revised Translation, with Introduction and Notes.* Edited and translated by Terrence N. Tice. Eugene, OR: Cascade Books, 2010. xxi, 114 pp. [Translation of 1826 edition with notes from 1806 edition.]

———. *Fifteen Sermons of Friedrich Schleiermacher Delivered to Celebrate the Beginning of a New Year.* Edited and translated by Edwina Lawler. Schleiermacher Studies and Translations 23. Lewiston, NY: Mellen, 2003. lxxxiii + 282 pp.

———. *Friedrich Schleiermacher on Creeds, Confessions and Church Union: That They May Be One.* Translated by Iain G. Nicol. Schleiermacher Studies and Translations 24. Lewiston, NY: Mellen, 2004. iii, 265 pp. [Includes nine items from 1817 and 1822, and 1831.]

———. *Introduction to Christian Ethics.* Translated by John C. Shelley. Nashville: Abingdon, 1989. 108 pp.

———. *The Life of Jesus.* Edited and with an Introduction by Jack C. Verheyden. Translated by S. Maclean Gilmour. Lives of Jesus Series. Philadelphia: Fortress, 1975. lxii + 481 pp.

————. *On Religion: Addresses in Response to Its Cultured Critics.* Translation of 1799, 1806 and 1821. Edited and translated by Terrence N. Tice. Richmond: John Knox, 1969. 383 pp. [A revised critical edition is to follow in 2020.]

————. *On Religion: Speeches to its Cultured Despisers.* Translation of 1799 ed. by Richard Crouter. Texts in German Philosophy. Cambridge: Cambridge University Press, 1988. xii, 231 pp.

————. *On the Doctrine of Election: With Special Reference to the Aphorisms of Dr. Bretschneider.* Translation with an introduction and notes by Iain G. Nicol and Allen G. Jorgenson. Foreword by Terrence N. Tice. Columbia Series in Reformed Theology. Louisville: Westminster John Knox, 2012. xii + 103 pp.

————. *On What Gives Value to Life.* Translated and edited by Edwina G. Lawler and Terrence N. Tice. Schleiermacher Studies and Translations 14. Lewiston, NY: Mellen, 1995. 112 pp. [An 1892/93 essay.]

————. *Reformed but Ever Reforming: Sermons in Relation to the Celebration of the Handing Over of the Augsburg Confession (1830).* Translated by Iain G. Nicol. Schleiermacher Studies and Translations 8. Lewiston, NY: Mellen, 1997. 185 pp. [Nine sermons (1830) on the three-hundredth anniversary of the Augsburg Confession's being handed over to the king.]

————. *Schleiermacher als Mensch; sein Werden und Wirken. Familien- und freundesbriefe.* Edited by Heinrich Meisner. 2 vols. Gotha: Perthes 1922–1929. 368 pp. (vol. 1) and 416 pp. (vol. 2).

————. *Schleiermachers Briefwechesel mit seiner Braut.* Edited by Heinrich Meisner. Gotha: Perthes, 1919. 414 pp.

————. *Schleiermacher's Soliloquies: An English Translation of the Monologen.* Translation of 1800, 1806 and 1826 editions intermixed, edited by Horace L. Friess. Chicago: Open Court, 1926. Reprint, Eugene, OR: Wipf & Stock, 2002. 238 pp. [A new ET of 1806 and 1826 editions is forthcoming.]

————. *Selected Sermons of Schleiermacher.* Translated by Mary Wilson. Foreign Biblical Library part 5. London: Hodder & Stoughton, 1890. 451 pp.

————. *Selections from Friedrich Schleiermacher's "Christian Ethics."* Edited and translated by James M. Brandt. Library of Theological Ethics. Louisville: Westminster John Knox, 2011. 198 pp.

————. *Servant of the Word: Selected Sermons of Friedrich Schleiermacher.* Translated with an introduction by Dawn De Vries. Fortress texts in Modern Theology. Philadelphia: Fortress, 1987. x + 230 pp. [Years of delivery and publication of the eleven sermons are not supplied, from: 1. Dec. 12, 1890, SW II.7 (1836); 2. Dec. 25, 1810, SW II.7 (1836); 3. Dec. 10, 1820, SW II.2 (1826, 1833); 4. Mar. 18, 1821, SW II.2 (1834, 1843); 5. Easter, Apr. 8, 1833, SW II.2 (1834, 1843); 6. Nov. 1, 1817, SW II.4 (1834); 7. Apr. 19, 1824, SW II.2 (1826, 1834, 1843); 8. Mar. 4, 1821, SW II.4 (1834, 1844); 9. July 4, 1830, SW II.2 (1834, 1843); 10. Oct. 24, 1830, SW II.2 (1834, 1843); 11. May 29, 1791, SW II.7 (1836).]

Secondary Works

Bauer, Johannes. *Schleiermacher als patriotischer Prediger.* Studien zur Geschichte des neueren Protestantismus 4. Giessen: Töpelmann, 1908. xii + 364 pp.

Blackwell, Albert L. "Schleiermacher's Sermon at Nathanael's Grave." *Journal of Religion*, 57.1 (1977) 64.

Dierkes, Hans, et al., eds. *Schleiermacher, Romanticism, and the Critical Arts: A Festschrift in Honor of Hermann Patsch*. New Athenaeum 8. Lewiston, NY: Mellen, 2008. 437 pp.

Hagan, Anette I. "Divine Providence and Human Freedom in the Quest for Ecological Living." In *Schleiermacher and Sustainability: A Theology of Ecological Living*, edited by Shelli M. Poe, 61–77. Columbia Series in Reformed Theology. Louisville: Westminster John Knox, 2018.

Kelsey, Catherine L. *Schleiermacher's Preaching, Dogmatics, and Biblical Criticism: The Interpretation of Jesus Christ in the Gospel of John*. Princeton Theological Monograph Series 68. Eugene, OR: Pickwick Publications, 2007. xi + 188 pp.

———. *Thinking about Christ with Schleiermacher*. Louisville: Westminster John Knox, 2003. 126 pp.

Meckenstock, Günter. *Deterministische Ethik und kritische Theologie: Die Auseinandersetzung des Frühen Schleiermacher mit Kant und Spinoza 1789–1794*. Schleiermacher-Archiv 5. Berlin: de Gruyter, 1988. 244 pp. [References to his first collection of sermons (1801) are included; its ET is forthcoming.]

Nowak, Kurt. *Schleiermacher: Leben, Werk und Wirkung*. UTB. Göttingen: Vandehoeck & Ruprecht, 2001. 632 pp.

Peiter, Hermann. *Christliche Ethik bei Schleiermacher—Christian Ethics according to Schleiermacher: Gesammelte Aufsatze und Besprechungen—Collected Essays and Reviews*. Edited by Terrence N. Tice. Princeton Theological Monograph Series 134. Eugene, OR: Pickwick Publications, 2010. xxvii + 772 pp.

Poe, Shelli M. *Essential Trinitarianism: Schleiermacher as Trinitarian Theologian*. T. & T. Clark Explorations in Reformed Theology. London: Bloomsbury T. & T. Clark, 2017. 180 pp.

———, ed. *Schleiermacher and Sustainability: A Theology for Ecological Living*. Columbia Series in Reformed Theology. Louisville: Westminster John Knox, 2018. xlii, 149 pp.

Prozesky, Martin. "A Critical Examination of the Pietistic Element in the Religious Philosophy of Freiedrich Schleiermacher." PhD diss., University of Rhodesia, 1976.

Tice, Terrence N. *Schleiermacher*. Pillars in Theology Series. Nashville: Abingdon, 2006. xii + 95 pp.

———. *Schleiermacher: The Psychology of Christian Faith and Life*. Mapping the Tradition Series. Lanham, MD: Lexington Books/Fortress Academic, 2018. vii + 111 pp.

———. *Schleiermacher's Sermons: A Chronological Listing and Account*. Schleiermacher Studies and Translations 15. Lewiston, NY: Mellen, 1997. 181 pp. [Not superseded by KGA III: *Predigten*, the fourteen large volumes of which do contain material not known in 1997; these include some new sermons and sermon outlines.]

Vial, Theodore. *Schleiermacher*. Guides for the Perplexed 105. London: Bloomsbury, 2013. ix + 150 pp.

Wehrung, Georg. "Der Durchgang Schleiermachers durch die Brüdergemeine." *Zeitschrift für systematische Theologie* 4/2 (1926/1927) 192–210.

Scripture Index

Analytical Index
of Subjects and Concepts

Please note: 1) Herein "subjects" include major biblical figures and all names applied to Jesus there. 2) Also, subjects of special interest include a long section on Schleiermacher and immediate family members. 3) Finally, items mentioned in my Fortress Academic translation of his critically important 1820 Christmas sermon are embraced here for purposes of comparison (2018). All three elements are deemed to be part and parcel of each other.

Name Index

Adelung's Dictionary, 64n4
America, 14 P.S.
Anna, prophetess, 105, 109
Arndt, Andreas von, 13 P.S.
Arnim, Achim von, 13 P.S., 116
  P.S.
Arnim, Bettinna von
  (daughter), 116 P.S.

Bach, Johann Sebastian, 108n10
Bardwell, Janet, viii
Bauer, Johannes, 71n1, 118 P.S.
Beethoven, Ludwig, 108n10
Berlin, 13 P.S., 15 P.S., 118 P.S.
  Academy of Sciences, 113
    P.S.
  Breslau, Silesia, 1n1, 12 P.S.
  Brethren's sister-house in,
    116 P.S.
  Cathedral Church in, 1n1
  Charity General Hospital,
    2n3, 117 P.S.
  Church of the Triune God,
    2n3
  Dreifaltigkeitskirche, 2,
    106n9
  Hallesches Tor in, 81 P.S.
  Kannonier Strasse, 115 P.S.
  Singakademie in, 113 P.S.
  University of, 5n7, 34n1, 113
    P.S., 116 P.S.
  Wilhelm Strasse 73, 115 P.S.
Berliner Gesangbuch, 113 P.S.
Bethlehem, 109, 119, 124

Blackwell, Albert L., 60n20
Blair, Hugo, vii
Brandt, James M., 59 P.S.
Bretano family, 116 P.S.
  von, 13 P.S.

Carraher, Heather, viii

De Vries, 34n1
DeWette,W.M.L., 114 P.S.
Dilthey, Wilhelm, 11 P.S.
Dohna estate, von, 118 P.S.
  family 1, 16n1
Dreifaltigkeitskirche, 113 P.S.

Europe, 14 P.S.

Fawcett, Joseph, vii
Funk, Jeremy viii

Galilee, 85, 125
Germany, 106n9, 114 P.S.

Halle, University of, 5n7, 13
  P.S., 16n1, 117 P.S.
Hanson, K.C., viii
Hayden, 108n10
Hegel, Wilhelm Friedrich, 116
  P.S.
Heidelberg, 116 P.S.
Herrnhuter Brethren, 4n5, 14
  P.S., 116 P.S.
Herz, Henriette (Jette), 116 P.S.

CPSIA information can be obtained
at www.ICGtesting.com
Printed in the USA
LVHW110958260922
729300LV00013B/159

9 781532 667398